THE SEVEN SPIRITUAL STEPS OF DANCING SALSA

A practical guide to dance with your Spirit

ALEX SOSA

© Alex Sosa.
Copyright 2011, Alex Sosa.
All rights reserved. No part of this publication may be reproduced, stored in a retrieval system or transmitted in any form or by any means, electronic, mechanical, photo-copying, recording, or otherwise, without the prior written permission of the author.

This book is dedicated to the Spirit,
to my mother and family,
and to all the dancers and musicians
of our planet. All sounds and movements are
coming from the same nature.

Alex Sosa

Acknowledgments

I would like to express my gratitude to all the people that support me on my journey for writing this book, without your help this book will be still an idea.

I want to thank the Spirit for guiding me and giving me the opportunity to write this book.

Special gratitude to Beverly Acevedo. Never crossed my mind that the same person one day gave me a job in a restaurant will also be editing this book, thank you for your support. Everything happens for a reason.

Lynn Martin. Thank you for listening and helping me to put all the ideas together, although the book is finished I still miss the chatting.

Juan Acevedo. Thank you for your support and inspiration, and for keeping the Spirit of the music going around. You are a great dancer, a great musician, and a great singer.

Dean James. Thank you for also helping in the editing of this book and for your support. You are a great person and a great dancer.

Ray Dhir. Thank you for your help and support. You are a great friend.

Also I would like to thank all the people that in one way or another form part of this book. Dancers, musicians, and the Salsa dance community in general. I hope you enjoy this book and hope this book helps you to dance spiritually conscious, bringing more happiness to your life as it does to my.

..The person without the Spirit does not accept the things that come from the Spirit of God but considers them foolishness, and cannot understand them because they are discerned only through the Spirit...

(1 Corinthians 2:14, The Bible)

The Spirit does not has a nationality, and yet all nationalities are in the Spirit. It is the Spirit's desire to be heard through a musician; as well, it is its desire to move through a dancer. The Spirit wants to express itself through our bodies. The Spirit only wants to experience happiness, in love, peace and harmony between us.

Alex Sosa

*Like a painter with his brush,
a dancer paints the music with the movement of his body.*

Music and dance are the doors to the temple of the human Spirit.

---

*Music is the spiritual evolution of sound,
dance is the spiritual evolution of movement,
and rhythm is the harmony of the Spirit
with the human body in the eternal dance of creation.*

---

*Spiritual dancing is not just about moving your body to the music,
but also feeling the music with your heart, touching the music with your soul.*

When you ask for a dance, you are giving a dance.

---

*Salsa music and dance are the evolution of different cultures
toward harmony, unity, and love.*

---

*Sound and movement help you to change your emotional state;
music and dance help you to change your life forever.*

---

*Dance for yourself and you will change a life,
dance for others, and you will change the planet.*

Alex Sosa

Seven points to warm up.

First: *Remember at all times that you don't have two left feet. You are powerful beyond imagination. Be positive and confident about yourself.*

Second: *Be grateful for the creation of your body, and also for the possibility to be able to communicate through it and express your emotions dancing with other people. Enjoy your journey.*

Third: *Open your mind and see energy around you, with you, and inside you. Improve your dance with the understanding of yourself; knowing that you are energy, dance with your Spirit. Remember: $E=mc^2$ (everything is energy).*

Fourth: *Remember that your emotions are an energy system given to you to guide you to a personal realization, listen to them and be a happy dancer.*

Fifth: *Everything in the universe is interconnected and moving in synchronicity like a clock, and that is rhythm. Keep it that way, dance in Clave.*

Sixth: *We are humans. We are social beings by nature. Don't be shy and ask others for a dance, help others to decide asking them for a dance. Time gone is happiness gone.*

Seventh: *Become what you really want. Make people happy on the way to your happiness. Dancing for others is dancing with your Spirit.*

CONTENTS

Introduction 1

Part 1

Chapter 1 : Sound and movement 7

Chapter 2 : The power of Salsa music and dance 13

Chapter 3 : The Salsa music and dance spiritual evolution 17

Chapter 4 : The Clave (The heart of Salsa) 23

Chapter 5 : Dancing in couples 31

Chapter 6 : The Salsa dancer's tools 35

Chapter 7 : Water and music 41

Chapter 8 : The Success formula 45

Chapter 9 : The wheel (La rueda) 49

Part 2
The Seven Spiritual Steps Of Dancing Salsa 53

Chapter 10 : STEP 1 - The mind of the dancer (Mind your mind) 55

Chapter 11 : STEP 2 - The body of the dancer (The dance partner of your Spirit) 65

Chapter 12 : STEP 3 - The Spirit (The real dancer) 73

Chapter 13 : STEP 4 - The emotions of the dancer (Dance happy) 83

Chapter 14 : STEP 5 - The Rhythm (All together) 89

Chapter 15 : STEP 6 - Salsa is a social dance (Ask for a dance) 97

Chapter 16 : STEP 7 - The Salsa dancer's purpose (Dance for others) 105

Conclusion 103

Introduction

Introduction

A tree keeps its roots in the darkness, and gives its fruits in the light.

A tree gives its fruits in the light, but the seed from where it began to grow was in the darkness, and in the darkness remain the roots that had been supporting it since the beginning.

Alex Sosa.

I was born in Havana, Cuba, a country well-known for its fantastic music and dance; also for its beautiful and well formed white sand beaches and happy people, people that keep their music and dance always alive, changing and growing. Cuba, the largest island in the Caribbean, geographically located at the entrance of the Gulf of Mexico as a key to America. From a cultural point of view Cuba has been a very important platform for the Salsa music and many other genres to expand to the rest of America, and today have reached the whole world. This makes me think about the four aspects of the three-dimensional reality, which are: *movement, sound, colour, and shape*. These are the same aspects of the Caribbean region. The Caribbean is known for its colourful nature, vibrant music and many types of dance. It looks like Cuba was the perfect place for a fantastic mix between different cultures; cultures that made the creation of Salsa music and Salsa dance possible for us to enjoy today.

The purpose of this book is to guide Salsa dancers to have a conscious spiritual experience whilst dancing, bringing awareness of what is really happening inside the dancer's mind and body during that magical moment when the body is connected and moving to the rhythm of the music. It is to guide the dancer to not just dance with the body but to dance with the Spirit; at the end, it is the Spirit who moves our bodies.

In my years of searching and asking questions to many Salsa dancers about how do they feel at their peak of their emotional experiences whilst dancing to Salsa music; they will use words like: Freedom, happiness, peace and other positive words. However, many Salsa dancers do not know how to explain this feeling. They are not consciously aware of what is going on inside of them while they are dancing to Salsa music. They simply don't know where these feelings are really coming from. Is my intention that by the end of this book, you will understand where these positive feelings come

Introduction

from when dancing, and use it as a very powerful tool to personal happiness and to the happiness of others around you.

Everything that you will read in this book is based on personal experiences. We all have our own way of perceiving reality. And we also have different beliefs, but there are laws in the universe that no matter what our beliefs are they will never change. They do not change, but they can guide and help us with all of our experiences in life. For example; we have the law of gravity. We believe in the law of gravity because we see its effects. We do not see the law, but the effects are there to prove its existence. In the same way, there are other laws that operate in our world, but much of the time we are not aware of them, and because of this, we do not get the most positive experiences as we could.

It is beyond the scope of this book to speak about the origin of the Salsa music and dance from a geographic point of view. There is a lot of information about this topic that can be easily found.

Many studies that have been done about the origin of the Salsa music and dance are pointing its beginnings in Cuba, with the Cuban genre named Son, which is the foundation in which Salsa music was created. Cuban Son is the fusion of different type of dance and music from Europe and Africa. When we study the history and evolution of Salsa music and dance, we will discover a very interesting mix between many cultures, which is just the material reality of another more deeply spiritual necessity that made this creation possible.

Everything emerges from the Spirit, and everything goes back to the Spirit.

We can say that, in reality, this so energetic music and dance called Salsa has its roots in the Spirit of human beings. It is a universal music and dance of very high vibration that has brought a lot of happiness to the hearts of many people around the planet, from America to Japan, bringing unity and spirituality everywhere it is played and danced.

If we consider the long journey of Salsa music and its composition, we will realize why this genre is so famous all over the planet, and why many people

Introduction

from different countries are attracted to this music and dance. We can say that Salsa music is a universal expression of the human Spirit; all the musicians and dancers feed themselves from the same energy for their creations. The Spirit does not have a nationality, and yet all nationalities are in the Spirit. It is the Spirit desire to be heard through a musician, as well as its desire to move through a dancer. The Spirit only wants to express itself through our bodies. The Spirit wants to experience happiness, in love, peace and harmony between us.

As Plato the great philosopher once pointed:

> *"Music is for the soul, like gymnastic is for the body".*
> *Plato*

Some questions for you:

- Have you ever asked yourself what attracted you to Salsa music and dance for the first time?

- Why are you still feeling attracted to this energetic music and dance?

- Do you pay attention to the sensations, emotions or feelings you may experience while you are dancing Salsa?

- Are you experiencing any frustration with your family or your partner because they do not understand your interest for this music and dance?

- What really make people dance?

These and other questions have a space in the mind of many Salsa dancers who are attracted to this energetic type of dance as well as its music of such an intense vibration. Other dancers just follow their Spirit and experience a very high state of satisfaction and happiness, that can be amplified if the experience is conscious, and the dancer is aware of what is really happening in that magical moment of moving your body to the music.

Introduction

In the pages of this book, you will find the answers to these questions. This book can be used as a very powerful tool to explain to everyone you get in contact with, the reasons behind your feelings about this music and dance.

This book is the result of many years of observation, information, study and experiences, first in myself and later confirmed with many Salsa dancers and musicians around the world. The result took me to the decision of sharing this book with the rest of the Salsa dancers to help them to dance spiritually conscious, and with the musicians, for they to understand the real reasons for which we, the dancers, move our bodies to dance with their musical inspiration *(In Spirit)*.

Part 1
Chapter 1

Sound

and

movement

Sound and movement

Sound and movement help you to change your emotional state; music and dance help you to change your life forever.
Alex Sosa

*In the beginning God created the heaven and the earth. And the earth was without form, and void; and darkness was upon the face of the deep. And the Spirit of God **moved** upon the face of the waters.*
(Genesis 1:1, 1:2, The Bible).

*And God **said**, let there be light, and there was light.*
(Genesis 1:3, The Bible).

In the material universe everything is vibrating; and everything that vibrates will produce a sound as a consequence. According to the law of cause and effect which explains that every action generated has a cause and that action generated by that cause always produce an effect, we then can say that any vibration is a cause and the sound produced is one of its effect, vibration implies movement and in the material universe (One verse) we can not have movement without sound or sound without movement, sound and movement are two aspects *(Movement, sound, color, and shape)* of our physical reality, they are active components of any creation, when we speak to someone they can hear our voice because the vibrations of our vocal cords are reaching their ears and the brain translate this vibrations given them meaning for these sounds to be understood, this meaning is called language. If we look around us and pay attention to anything that is moving we will hear a sound, we can clap our hands or breath deeply and hear the sound of our hands or our breathing, we can hear the sound of a car's wheels passing by, the trees moving with the wind, the waves of the sea, everything that we see in movement will produce a sound, if we hear it or not the vibration of the sound is there. Human beings can only hear between about 20 Hz and 20,000 Hz (20 kHz). Many other species have different range of hearing. For instance; dogs can perceive the vibrations of sound higher than 20,000 Hz (20 kHz) which is the limit of the human hearing. Even the planets produce a sound in their rotation, and this is called the music of the spheres (By Kepler).

Sound and movement

Figure 1. When we read a musical writing, we are reading movements at the same time.

That is why many musical genres have their own type of dance; and sometimes you can see some new musical creation accompanied by a new type of dance to identify that particular music that has been created.

We find a particular way of dancing in almost every country in the planet. We can identify some countries because of their music and way of dancing, for instance, we have the Merengue music and dance from Dominican Republic, the Tango from Argentina, the Samba from Brazil, and the Cueca from Chile. In that way we can carry on naming many other countries and their music and dance which represent their culture.

In Salsa music, we found a peculiarity because we have different styles of dancing to the same music; and this shows the freedom that salsa music can produce in our consciousness and also the capacity of the human body to move with rhythm and in harmony in different ways with this type of music.

During the course of history human beings discovered that Sounds can be put into harmony and called music to this discovery, also humans discovered that music has a big influence in the state of our consciousness. We play music according to our emotional state. We have music for many different occasions, for instance, when we go to the cinema music and sounds are used in ways to get us to jump up screaming on our seat in a terror movie; or crying our eyes out in a very sad scene. The fact is that sound has the capacity to transform the matter, but sound in harmony, which we call music, has the capacity to move our Spirit.

Sound and movement

We have sounds of high vibration and low vibration in the sound scale, and according to the vibration, it will be the effect caused to the matter *(Also our body)*, in terms of music we have songs that make us feel in one way; and others that do not go so deep, everyone can experience this, in Salsa music we have some particular songs that make us dance all night changing our emotional state, keeping us happily dancing, and in that moment, our consciousness is transforming our physical or material body, in that moment of happiness that emotional energy of great joy is making our brain produce chemical reactions that bring good health to our body.

In the universe, everything is constantly moving and transforming, even if you take a seat and close your eyes and don't move at all still your heart will be working to keep you alive. All your organs carry on working independently of your decision of been still, also your mind will produce different thoughts whilst you are in that position of stillness, in the universe everything is in some way dancing with everything else, it is a principle of the core of nature to move, to manifest itself in this way through movement and sound. We find different music and dances in nature. We find music in the trine of the birds, in the wolf calling the rest of the herd, as well as in the sea we find the dolphins jumping and singing very happily in front of a visitor. In nature we find many kinds of dances, in the animal Kingdom many animals dance around their partners to show their interest; we can see how the wind dances with the trees and with the sea producing the waves, also our planet earth is rotating around the sun like in an eternal dance; energy has constantly been expressed in nature in different forms of movements and sounds and when they are placed in harmony we call it music and dance.

The universe is like a synchronized orchestra than in a very impressive way is playing its own music and dancing its own dances, orchestra in which we, the human beings; form part as another musician or another dancer. We all form part of an eternal and beautiful show called creation.

Chapter 2

The power of Salsa music and dance

The power of Salsa music and dance

Salsa Music and dance have the capacity to unite people; music goes deeper into the human soul and can change a person's life forever, making that person feel happy in a way that will then desire to share that happiness dancing with others.

Alex Sosa.

In a Salsa club, the dance floor does not separate the dancers from the musicians' stage. They are in the right place united by the music; the music takes the message from the musicians to the dancers. The music is the envelope in which the message of the inspiration *(in Spirit)* of the musicians can travel to the body of the dancer and in that way musicians and dancers become one in love and harmony, in the same way that the different notes become one in harmony in the song being played; in that same way musicians and dancers are not separated beings, at the spiritual level. They are one having the same experience, and the dancers' bodies in the physical plane are the instruments with which they can touch and play with the music in harmony, like the musicians' instruments together playing the music in harmony for them to dance. They receive and give energy to each other, taking each other to a higher vibration and a happy emotional state.

We can say today that Salsa music and dance had brought unity to our planet. People from many countries go to Salsa congresses or any Salsa events to dance with other people of different nationalities that they had never met before, and in that magic moment salsa music and dance are the only languages they need to speak to understand each other, just by extending their arms asking for a dance as a way also of giving someone else a dance in return.

A little story with a big meaning:
I remember once working in a restaurant on valentine's day that we received a lovely couple that wanted to eat that night like many other couples that booked for that particular night, with the difference that this couple were blind, they both couldn't see, one member of the staff had to read the menu to this beautiful couple, and many people around them were moved by the nice feeling of them going out together on valentine's day to share their love for each other, but something magical happened when the musician started playing, and the music reached the couple's hears, the lady of that couple started moving her body in her chair, she started to dance in the chair and

The power of Salsa music and dance

moving her head to the music very passionate, she knew her limitation for dancing on her feet because her condition and the place, but that did not stop her from having a wonderful time dancing in her chair and feeling the music inside her, her husband explained later that he knew her love and passion for music and he heard about this restaurant and the good music played every week, and he wanted to give her that present for valentines day, they had a fantastic night and she was so happy and promised to go back again.

This is a very moving example of the power of music and dance, and how music transforms us inside bringing happiness to our soul, no matter the conditions of the body.

Today information is everywhere with the internet connecting people's minds, today borders between countries are irrelevant. We are more connected than ever mentally and this makes us have a faster impulse to evolve, to unite the whole planet as a big family. This is why we go to Salsa congresses and enjoy so much to share dancing and keeping contact with new friends and also to know about new activities, parties, congresses and festivals; because although we are mentally connected trough the internet, we, as humans, still need physical and social contact, because we are social beings, and because we need physically to interact and experience with each other for our spiritual growth and our evolution, and Salsa music and dance have proven to be a very good way to help to achieve this unity and social harmony of humanity.

Chapter 3

The Salsa music and dance spiritual evolution

The Salsa music and dance spiritual evolution

Salsa music and dance are the evolution of different cultures toward harmony, unity and love.
Alex Sosa.

The soul does not evolve in isolation. The soul evolves trough cultural interaction. A child in isolation does not evolve. He needs culture to develop. Human beings are social beings by nature.

Salsa music and dance, as many people will agree, have been the result of many years of interactions between Europeans and Africans cultures in the Caribbean and in America in general. When we study the beginnings of the Salsa music and dance we will find the long journey of this dance, and we will realize the beautiful evolution of this mix of cultures that took place throughout history.

In terms of evolution, we know that for something to evolve, or change, it will have to give up a previous form, shape, or concept, and this normally happens as a result of the adaptability to the new environment, in order to survive, which means that reality in each moment of the evolution is demanding harmony, adaptability, or balance between different poles of energies *(In terms of Salsa music and dance, there was an energetic balance in the mix of the different cultures, that form part of this type of music and its dance).*

In the history and evolution of Salsa music and dance, we can find the journey through many countries, since the country dance in UK was taken to France *(Contredanse)* and onto Spain *(Contradanza)*, later we find the arrival in the Caribbean and the mix with the African rhythms throughout the years to become the Cuban Son. Later, we know that once again, this rhythm called Son, went from the country side to reach the Cities, and carry on the evolution mixing with new ways of dancing, and new instruments. Then, when the Cuban revolution took place, many musicians left the country and went to US, and it was in US when the Salsa word was finally introduced in the evolution of this music and dance, taking this big mix between cultures, to a new level in its evolution, back to Europe, Africa and the rest of the planet.

The Salsa music and dance spiritual evolution

Today, we find salsa music and dance every where in the world, but we want to explain to you the evolution of this music and dance from a spiritual point of view, which is very similar to the history or its physical evolution.

We need to imagine the physical world from the energy point of view. Energy is always changing, always moving in a circle, always dancing in harmony reaching for a higher level of development, and this is called evolution *(E=Energy, Volution=Growing)*. If you noticed we cannot stop progress, progress is always happening around us. If we look at the history of our planet and our humanity we will see that we are more mixed than ever, we depend more and more economically from the rest, and in terms of music, we see this happening in many genres of music, many genres exist because of this mix between cultures, and this is the case of Salsa music and dance, it is an evolution of different cultures that merged with each other through history trying to run away from pain and into happiness, freedom and harmony. Leaving the old structure and assimilating the new one; and in that process many cultures were unified creating a new blend or new culture. There is a logic to follow in terms of feelings that is guiding us into a higher level of organization and harmony, and that is only possible because in the deepest of our being we are pure consciousness, and when connected to the highest one is pulled toward the more organized, and more well defined harmony. We are finding slowly who we really are, and music and dancing are a very important key for this revelation to take place. Music and dance have been with us since the very beginning, since the first sound or instrument made by men, until today's most sophisticated instruments and singing and dancing techniques. We have been mixing our cultures and in that process developing our physical reality with the help of our music and dance, with our cultural interconnection, and in this process Salsa music and dance brought a lot of these changes into humanity. This means that we are growing from apparently many small and separated beings into a bigger, more unified, and harmonious one, ruled by the law of pure love.

We can say today that from a spiritual evolution point of view Salsa music and dance are the result of the mix, balance or unity between the Spirit of the human beings of this beautiful planet, we can say that Salsa music and dance, are the Spirit of the European culture mixed with the Spirit of the African culture, that in an evolutionary journey, came to become Salsa

The Salsa music and dance spiritual evolution

Music and dance in the Caribbean and in America, going back to Europe, Africa and the rest of the planet, closing the circle as a new and evolved mix of sounds and many stiles of dancing. In this evolution, we find how energy, in order to balance itself, looking for harmony, came up with new creations for us to experience, the more we interact with each other in the spiritual level, the more we evolve, because this is the nature of the Spirit, and this is what we are. Energy evolving constantly to illuminate all beings.

Chapter 4

The clave
(The heart of Salsa)

The clave *(The heart of Salsa)*

"Evolution is the law of Life. Number is the law of the Universe. Unity is the law of God"
Pythagoras

The Clave *(In Spanish: La Clave)* is the backbone and the heart of the Salsa music; it is what keeps the Salsa music alive and guides all the instruments to play in harmony around it. In the same way your rhythmic heart with its beats keeps all the organs receiving blood, to keep functioning properly and in harmony with each other, to keep your body alive. Or the Sun created in the centre of our solar system, keeping the planets rotating around it. In the same way, the Clave pattern is the centre of the Salsa music and dance. It is the base that keeps holding the rhythm together. All the instruments play around the Clave pattern in total harmony with its compass, and all the musicians are constantly aware of the Clave pattern to keep the rhythm alive, and the Salsa dancers are also aware of this pattern in order to keep with the rhythm on the dance floor.

In Salsa music, the Clave is commonly played in a pattern of *(three strokes + two strokes, for Son)* or *(two strokes + three strokes, for Rumba)* sequence, which is called (The Cuban Clave). It is called the Cuban Clave, because it is the Clave of the Cuban Son, and the Cuban Son is the foundation in which Salsa was created.

This mathematical sequence in the Clave pattern of *(3 strokes + 2 strokes)* is very important to know, because this sounds like proportions, hold the key for which we are attracted to this music and dance. This mathematical sequence, is found to be used by nature to build everything in the material universe, *(including the human body)*; with the golden spiral, a logarithmic spiral, which is the shape of the cochlea of the inside ear, and It is also the shape of ram's horns, snail shells, and the form of galaxies, and this is the reason for which we are attracted naturally to this pattern.

The Clave pattern is an energy that keeps the rest of the musical instruments in harmony; it is a vibration that expresses beauty in sound, and human beings are creatures made to search, find, admire, and enjoy the beauty.

The clave (The heart of Salsa)

We are creators of beauty, and we identify beauty through our five senses, because that is what we are inside, beauty is what our essence is, and the Clave instrument, which is played with our hands, always keeps the Salsa music alive, because of the mathematical proportions in terms of sound.

In Africa, Asia and Europe, we can find many forms of Clave patterns, which tell us that the Clave is like the core or centre of any musical composition, of many cultures, but in the deepest reality, it is all about the mathematics and numbers that are behind the patterns of any musical composition.

It is not by chance that some people are attracted to Salsa music and dance. One of the reasons is the mathematical pattern in this music. Human beings have five physical senses and through our five physical senses, we perceive our reality, and we are attracted or not to that which we consider harmonious, pleasant or beautiful. For instance, we have a particular attraction to some types of food according to our taste and experiences that we have had before, the same happens with our smell when we like a particular perfume or aftershave, or with our sight when we look at beauty in front of us in many ways, could be a beautiful painting or a person. The fact is that we are attracted to our external world trough our five physical senses, and this is what happen with music, and in this case with Salsa music.

Pythagoras, father of numbers:

According to Pythagoras, in the universe everything is based in numbers, proportions and dimensions, and man is the measure of all things, because it is inside us that everything takes meaning. If we look to our body, we can see that the body is divided in two arms, two legs and so on, the same applies to everything else in nature, in the three-dimensional plane everything has temperature, dimensions and proportions, color and shape, and the relation or harmony between this proportion will produce an effect inside us through our senses, for instance, we see a person beautiful because there is a mathematical harmony between shape and proportions, the same in a painting between colors, dimensions and proportions, and we call beauty to this feeling that attracts us to this visual harmony. In Salsa music, we find the same attraction through our ears because the mathematical harmony of the vibrations of the different sounds of the musical instruments playing around

The clave *(The heart of Salsa)*

the Clave pattern and the same happens with the Salsa dance. The patterns are felt in the body elevating the vibration and making the body move with the same Clave pattern. In few words, we can say that, musicians play Salsa in Clave and dancers dance Salsa in Clave too.

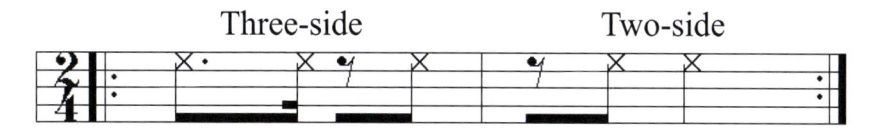

Figure 2. *Son clave in two measures of 2/4*

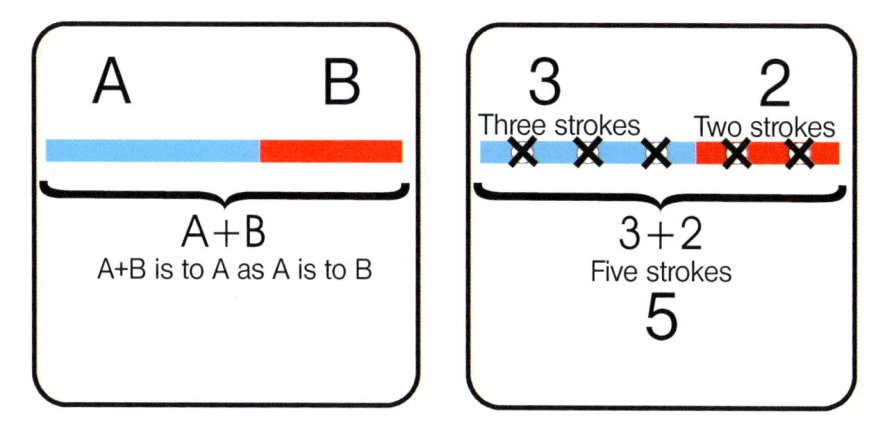

Figure 3. *The golden section.*   **Figure 4.** *The five-strokes Clave pattern.*

The golden section is a line segment divided according to the golden ratio: The total length a + b is to the length of the longer segment a as the length of a is to the length of the shorter segment b. In mathematics and the arts, two quantities are in the golden ratio if the ratio of the sum of the quantities to the larger quantity is equal to the ratio of the larger quantity to the smaller one. The golden ratio is an irrational mathematical constant, approximately 1.6180339887 (**From Wikipedia, the free encyclopedia**)

The clave *(The heart of Salsa)*

In Salsa music, the Clave patter posses some of the Fibonacci series of numbers *(phi) (1+1+2+3+5+8+13+21+34+55+89+144...)*, this series of numbers is found everywhere in nature. This series of numbers is like a code that nature uses to build everything in the material plane. It is like a code for beauty and harmonious evolution. This series of numbers is found inside our bodies, and outside us, everywhere in nature. Also in the architecture of the Ancient Greek, and in terms of sound like these numbers *(2,3,5)* found in the Clave pattern, are the essence of the music, is like the DNA of the Salsa music, and in that pattern our ears recognize a mathematical harmony that once it has reached our brain will become spiritual beauty, only the Spirit inside us can determine when beauty is present, and that only happens when the harmony outside us moves the spiritual emotion inside us, we are the container of the beauty and in Salsa music, the Clave pattern is the mathematical harmony that wakes up that spiritual emotion inside us.

The Numbers in the Clave:
In numerology every number from 1 to 9 has a meaning, the number 2 is the first female number and the number 3 the first male number been the number 5 the union between 2 and 3, in the Clave instrument we also have two peace of wood, one is called the female and the other the male, the male Clave is the one that we use to stroke the female Clave in patterns of 3 and 2 to create the Clave pattern of the 5 strokes, the number five is a very important number, it is a number that expresses freedom because it is the number that is in the middle between the other numbers and according to the law of rhythm in nature everything that is inside must come out and everything that is down must go up, and in terms of evolution freedom is a key factor for the development process to occur, our Spirit inside wants to express itself, and experience the physical world trough us, and for doing this we have five physical senses *(number 5)* to experience and understand reality around us; in order to do this human beings have created sciences along with arts and moral ethics, sciences help us understand our exterior or material world, the arts are our tools to express our internal beauty in different ways and moral ethics guide us to achieve justice, to create a balanced environment. All of this forms our culture, and it is through culture that we develop as human beings and Salsa music and dance are the result of the mix of different cultures always seeking freedom and harmony, this is what people say they feel on the dance floor.

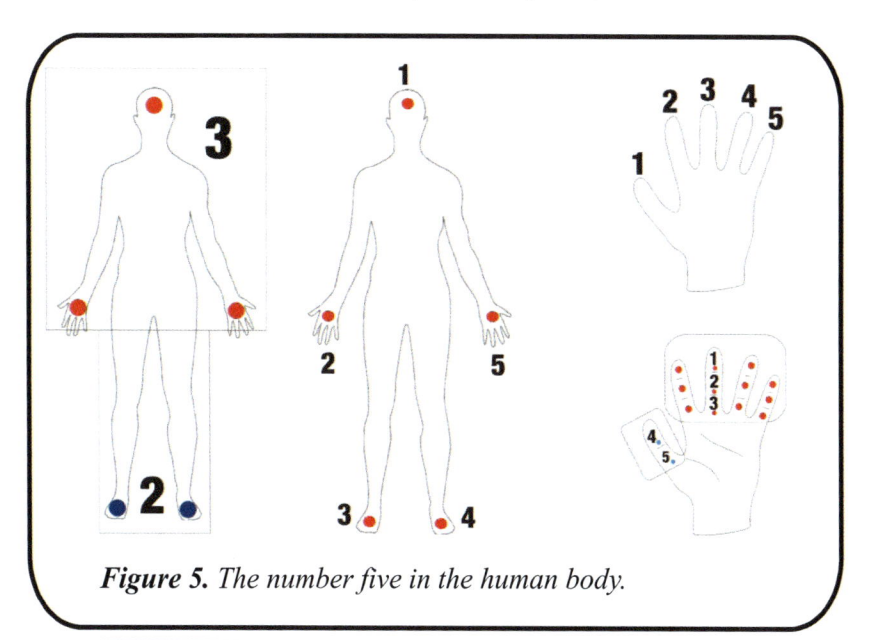

The clave *(The heart of Salsa)*

Figure 5. The number five in the human body.

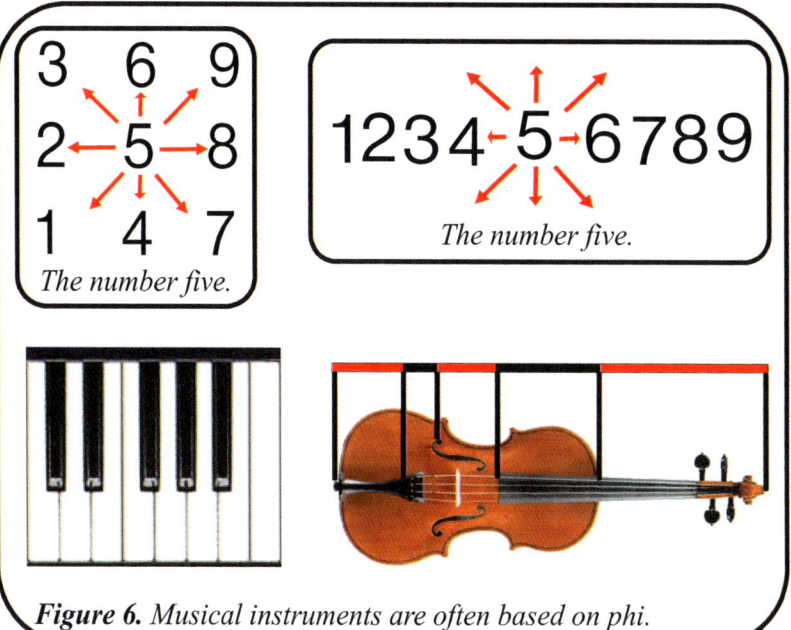

The number five.

The number five.

Figure 6. Musical instruments are often based on phi.

~29~

The clave *(The heart of Salsa)*

We see this mathematical proportion in our body; this is something that Da Vinci explained in **The Vitruvian man**, when he explained about the human body proportions, he knew about the effect of the proportions in the human eye and applied this to his paintings. We are supposed to be the link between God and the material universe, between Spirit and matter. We are the creature that was given the mind and intellect to create, and to bring harmony into the planet; harmony means the balance or middle way, and it is the number **5** the number in that middle. We are the microcosms according to Pythagoras, and if we look to our body, we can see that we have the number **5** in us. For instance, we have **5** fingers in our hands and feet, and our fingers on our hands are divided in **3** and **2** sections. We also have five physical senses. In music, we have the pentagram where we write the music, and if we look at the piano instrument, we can see the keys divided by sections of **3** and **2** black keys.

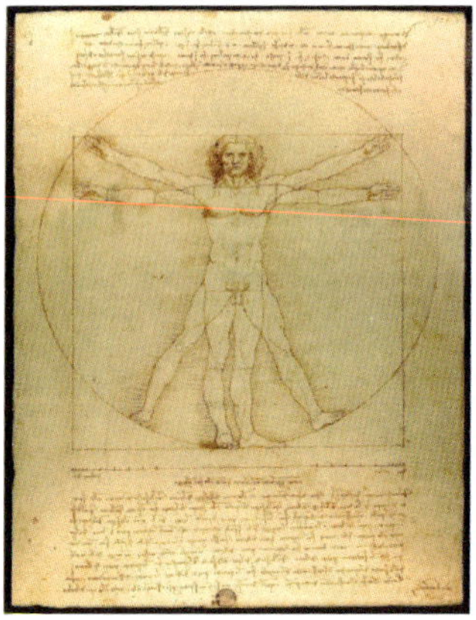

Figure 7. The Vitruvian Man is a world-renowned drawing created by Leonardo da Vinci circa 1487.

The drawing and text are sometimes called the Canon of Proportions or, less often, Proportions of Man.

(From Wikipedia, the free encyclopedia)

The word music came from the Greek musique, which means muse. Many musicians believe that their moments of creation only happen when some muse inspired them, according to mysticism the muse is the link between the divine plane and our material plane. The muse is the one that is supposed to bring knowledge to humans in order to maintain the evolution toward the unity to the divine.

In conclusion, the Clave pattern is the mathematical structure that holds the Salsa music together and also the guide for the dancers to keep the rhythm going in their bodies in harmony with the music. The Clave pattern is the voice and movement of freedom in the creation.

Chapter 5

Dancing in couples
(An act of creation)

Dancing in couples

Dancing in couples it is an act of creation.
Alex Sosa.

Salsa dance like Tango or many other types of dance are meant to be danced in couples, dancing in couples is not just about a man and a woman dancing together to have a good time, dancing in couples it is an act of creation, where the man leads the woman and guides her to complete the turns around him. Every turn finish brings with it a deep sense of happiness to the couple dancing, and this happens repeatedly until the music is finished leaving the couple in total satisfaction.

In the universe, there are two energies that take place in any creation, these two energies are masculine *(Yang)* and feminine *(Yin)*. These two energies are present in any act of creation, where masculine energy initiates the action, and the feminine energy materializes as the work.

We can see these energies manifested in nature, with the Sun being the masculine energy *(Yang)*, and the Earth the feminine energy *(Yin)*. We can experience in the winter when the Sun gets separated from the Earth, how the trees lose their leafs, and the grass stops from growing and everything seems to slow down, and in the spring, when the Earth and the Sun are coming closer, and everything starts to get green again and life manifested all over the Earth. This happens in the macrocosm's level and in the microcosm's level also with the Atom formed by electrons, protons and their interaction creating the elements, to form molecules and later the cells and then organs of living beings.

In Salsa dance, the man must know the turns to initiate them, and guide the woman through the dance, and the woman should know which the man intentions are, and follow his guidance helping each other to complete each turn, in order to work together to achieve mutual satisfaction in the dance. In terms of energy, the dancing couples *(Yin/Yang)* are creating the dance. They are physically manifesting the turns. And they are spiritually, creating happiness. They are inspired by the positivity of that moment.

I always like to associate the Salsa dance with the four seasons of our planet *(Spring, Summer, Autumn, and Winter)*, I like to associate the dance with the

Dancing in couple

four seasons because it is through the four seasons that everything is created in our planet, each season brings it's own beauty and each season has a reason to exist and I associate this with the dance because I believe that the same happens in the Salsa clubs at the moment when the music starts and the couple get together on the dance floor, that moment for me is like *(The Spring season)* of the dance and the pick moment of satisfaction in the dance as *(The Summer)* of the dance, then when the dance finished with the music and the couple separate and the vibration slows down is *(The Autumn)* of the dance, and they may go and take a seat to rest, that moment for me is *(The Winter)* of the dance, and the next time they go back to the dance floor for another dance the same begins again, exactly as the seasons of our beautiful planet, each moment creates the next one, and one gives meaning to the other, and in the process the dance is created, in that same way the Salsa dance has been evolving during many years together with the evolution of our humanity. Also many Salsa dancers like to keep dancing all night because their love and passion for the music and the enjoyment of the feeling they experience in that moment of the dance that I like to call the Summer of the dance, and in reality, although we need the Winter *(To rest)* to balance our nature, we always are looking forward for the Summer to arrive, to elevate our vibration and celebrate the Spirit.

Chapter 6

The Salsa dancer's tools

The Salsa dancer's tools

A good student, goes to school with everything he or she may need to use for the learning process, from this depends the learning, and the graduation at the end of his studies, in the same way a good mechanic depends of his tools to do a good job, in this same way the Salsa dance student depends on his tools to achieve his purpose without any dilate. These tools are divided in two groups. In one group, we have the material tools and in the other group we have the spiritual tools. The material tools are the tools that the Salsa dance student can see and touch. The spiritual tools are the tools that the Salsa dance student cannot see or touch with his physical body. These tools can only be felt and sensed through the consciousness.

Here are the tools, and an explanation of them.

Material tools:
1 - Body
2 - Teacher
3 - Dressing
4 - Shoes
5 - Music
6 - Water

Spiritual tools:
1 - Mind
2 - Emotions
3 - Intention
4 - Attention
5 - Spirit

Explanation of the tools:

Body: The body is the vehicle that the Spirit uses to express itself on the dance floor. The body is the house in which we really always live. It is important to take care of it with a good diet, and good breathing exercises, to oxygenate it properly. Our body will respond back to us with the same love we treat it.

The Salsa dancer's tools

Teacher: The Salsa teacher must be selected with care, for a few reasons. One reason is that we are dedicating a percentage of our finances to learn how to dance, and we want to make sure we are in good hands. Other reasons are, time that we don't really want to waste, and the style. There is many Salsa Stiles you can learn, but for a beginner, it is better to choose one style that you feel comfortable with, and develop this style first.

Dressing: The dressing is another very important factor that we must care about. It is important that once in the class nothing takes our attention away from making us feel uncomfortable. We all want to look good in front of other people, but it is also important that the body has comfort and freedom of movement, and the dressing should provide just that.

Shoes: The shoes like the dressing are very important because this is about dancing Salsa, and in Salsa dance you find your body moving constantly and turning in many directions and sometimes very fast, which means that your shoes must be comfortable and adjust to your feeds to avoid any problems that can dilate your learning.

Music: Music is very important; music wakes up our Spirit and puts us to dance. We have music for different occasions, like weddings, birthdays, funeral, etc. Each music we listen, will have an effect on us. Music makes us feel emotions. It has the power to enter the unconscious mind and bring out memories of the past. It is very important, dancing to the music we like, to enjoy the experience.

Water: During any physical activity, our body loses water when sweating, dancing Salsa will make you sweat, and will be good for your body to recover this water, try keeping a bottle of water with you in classes and in the Salsa clubs to keep your body in balance.

Now the Spiritual tools explained:

Mind: It is important for a Salsa student to use the mind with care. We become what we think about ourselves regularly, if we want to learn to dance Salsa, we must think positive, Salsa is a positive, and very energetic dance, keeping the right attitude, and the right use of the mind will give you a very

The Salsa dancer's tools

powerful positive feeling of self-confidence, and you will accelerate your learning process in a very happy state.

Emotions: After your mind produces a thought you will have a feeling about that thought, and this feeling will bring out an emotion, your emotions have a beginning in the mind, but sometimes we do not pay attention to our thoughts, and our emotions will call for our attention, we must listen to our emotions and see what they are trying to tell us, if we feel bad it means that something is not going right, find the problem, fix it, and keep evolving toward your goal, you will have some days better than others but that is ok, it is the law of rhythm of the universe but your emotions will guide you through your journey, listen to them and dance happily.

Intention: Your intention is your final goal. It is your treasure waiting to be collected, once you have decided that you want to become a Salsa dancer. You must keep focusing in that intention. That intention is your point of reference and to that point you are walking in each Salsa class, in each move learned, every time you think that you are not growing toward your goal, or you feel that your energies are getting weak it could be possible that your intention has been abandoned, or you are not dedicating enough time to your intention. Ask yourself if still is this what you really want and if the answer is positive, get back to focus in your intention, and that will give you the energy missing to carry on. Your intention is like a rope. Keep pulling the rope until you arrive at your destination. Remember that everything we dedicate time and effort will grow strong, and everything that we do not dedicate time and effort to, will simply dissipate. It is a law.

Attention: While your intention is to focus on what you want (To become a Salsa dancer), your attention must be focused on what you are becoming, pay attention to each move that you are learning in the class, each step and each holding of hands. Do not get lazy with this, remember that in just one second of distraction your body can suffer a lesion, and this will dilate your intention, your goal. Your intention depends of your attention in each moment of your journey. You must keep focusing.

The Salsa dancer's tools

Spirit: Your Spirit is nothing else that the real dancer, yourself. It is the Spirit which makes the initial call to learn this dance, when, for some reason. You get in contact with this music or dance. Once your Spirit identifies itself with this vibration it will keep telling you to move in that direction, it will be looking for happiness, balance, harmony and life in this music and dance, all the tools depend on the Spirit to move, and the Spirit depends of these tools to dance, to feel free and happy on the dance floor, experiencing the reality of the dance moment. Everything in the universe is dancing with everything else, if your Spirit makes the call, listen to it, and follow the energy dancing spiritually.

Chapter 7

Water and music

Water and music

*And the Spirit of God **moved** upon the face of the waters.*
(Genesis 1:2, The Bible)

According to scientists water is the source of all forms of biological life on our planet. A big portion of the mass of our body is made of water. The same applies to our planet. If we compare our body with our planet we will find a very close similarity. For instance, the largest part of the mass of our planet is water, we see this in the oceans and the rivers that form this beautiful planet. In our body, we can see this pattern because the majority of the mass is water also, water is vital for our existence, for our body functions. Our body's rivers are our arteries, and veins, our body and our planet have a common destiny. We are one and the same.

Water is the only substance that can exist in three stages: *Solid, liquid, and gas*, and it is also the only substance that can expand when it is cold. According to the discovery of the Doctor Massaru Emoto, which explains that water has memory and has the capacity to change its structure according to the sound to which it is exposed. In the same way the Sun has a sound frequency which when reaches our planet will determinate the movement and structure of everything on Earth. Then, we can say that, sound has the capacity to structure the water of our body, in Salsa music, we have the case where Salsa music makes us feel happy while dancing, and this happiness, is responsible, together with the music, for the structure of our body's cells, for the molecules of water to be shaped in beautiful forms, bringing health to our whole body. When sound transforms matter; music, which has the harmony and beauty of different sounds coming together, has the capacity to heal our body, to make us feel inspired. And we are talking about a big percentage of our body.

There is a link between the Sun and our heart. In astrology, the sign of Leo is associated with the heart, and in fact, a person who is born under this sign, is always recommended to take care of the blood circulation system and the heart through their emotions. It is very important to know that our minds, through our thoughts will dictate our state of being. And since our body mass is mainly water, and water has memory, and the capacity to shape and change according to our emotions and the sounds around us, then, it will be very important for our health to expose ourselves to the music we really like, and to dance elevating our vibration with the happiest music we can find.

Water and music

Furthermore, it is very important to feel appreciation on the dance floor, for the musicians playing the music we are dancing, and that very feeling of sending love to the musicians, and to the person dancing with us, will increase our vibration, our spirituality, and our health too.

Chapter 8

The Success formula

The Success formula

$$S = MA^2$$

Success: Be, Enjoy, Have, Live

Mind: Believe, Think, Desire, Know, Plan

Action: Become, Do, Move, Build, Make, Create, Express, Manifest, Change, Practice, Produce

Figure 8. The Success formula.

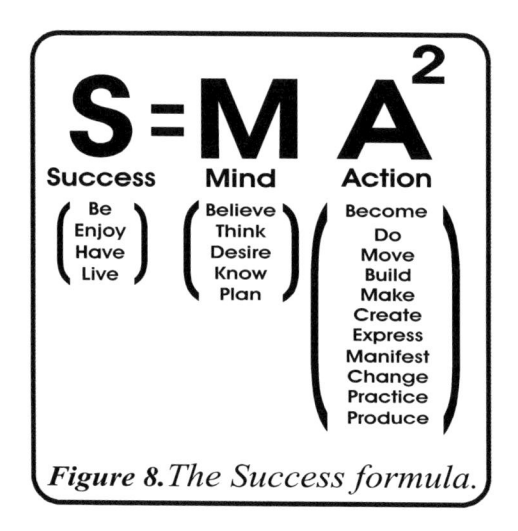

This simple formula, is just to help you understand the importance of taking action, and practice to become what you really want, using your mind to organize the ideas, and the body as the tool to make it happen.

As Albert Einstein explained in his formula $(E = mc2)$, in the material universe everything is energy, and energy can be transformed if the speed of light in it changes. In the same way, we can transform our lives if we desire to do so, because we are energy.

Success is a very big word. It means many things to different people, but in essence, success is what we really want in every aspect of our life.

In this formula S= MA2, S=Success, M=Mind, A2=Lot of Action.

Explanation of the formula:

In the Einstein formula *(E)* stand for *(Rest mass energy)*, and explain that everything is energy in the universe. In the formula that I suggest to you, *(S)* stand for *(Success)*, and success is all around you, and can be attracted to any area of your life. You just need to desire it, strongly enough to move toward it.

The Success formula

In the Einstein formula, *(M)* stands for *(Mass)*, explaining, that mass is energy at rest. In the formula that I suggest to you, *(M)* stands for *(Mind)*, because before someone becomes successful, it has to use the mind, to organize and plan every detail of the journey to that success.

In the Einstein formula *(C2)* stands for *(Speed of light in a vacuum)*, explaining that if the speed of light in any mass changes. Then the mass will be transformed. In the formula that I suggest to you, *(A2)* stand for *(Lot of Action)*, because without action any planning or thinking does not have meaning in the three-dimensional world, and the more action you take, the more success you can achieve.

What can you do with this formula?

You can place this formula where you can see it regularly, in order to remind you the importance of taking action, and to give you inspiration, to take that action every time you look at it.

So, if you desire to become a successful Salsa dancer, or even if you already are a Salsa dancer, and would like to improve your dance skills and get better and better every day, then remember this formula and keep taking action.

Never forget that the mind moves the body and in any moment of your journey you make feel like stopping, this means you may need a rest to carry on later, or you may got in the comfort zone. Ask yourself the question: Am I taking enough and the right actions toward my goals?. This simple question will bring your awareness back to continue guiding you to your success.

Chapter 9

The wheel
(Dancing in the wheel)

The wheel (Dancing in the wheel)

In the universe, energy moves in circles.

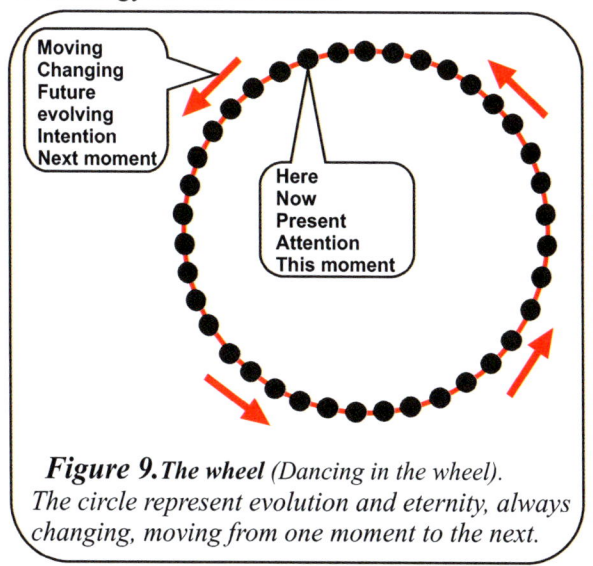

Figure 9. The wheel (Dancing in the wheel). The circle represent evolution and eternity, always changing, moving from one moment to the next.

Dancing in the wheel is characteristic of the Cuban style. Some couples gathering together forming a circle on the dance floor. It is called the wheel, because during the dance, the couples change partners constantly, moving onto the next dancer, going around in a circle. In terms of geometry, a circle and the sphere are perfect forms which signify eternity, always turning like the planets. For instance, the Earth is a sphere that is moving (rotating) in a circled direction, constantly around the Sun. The same happens on a small scale when we look at an electron moving around the nucleus of an atom, and this is what happens in the Salsa wheel.

When we are dancing Salsa, we are moving around our partner, and going around in the wheel. In nature, we find this round shape in many living beings. We find this round shape in many fruits, like oranges, apples, grapes, and more. Even some instruments, have the area of contact to produce the sound in a round shape. Like for instance, the maracas, drums, bongos, etc. Also in our five senses, if we look to our eyes, we will see that they are roundly shaped too.

Our ears are roundly shaped also. The same happens if we look to our nose,

The wheel (Dancing in the wheel)

and mouth, and even more, if we look at our finger tips, we will see how they have been designed roundly, we can say that our five senses are roundly shaped to experience eternity, which is how feels like, when we are experiencing a very powerful and happy moment of fun dancing in the wheel. In this moment, we experience a very powerful feeling of happiness, and sometimes, when the music stopped playing, we do not want to stop dancing. We are moving in a circle, and every turn is a moment of creation that we enjoy and pass to the next one, like one day is followed by the next, created by the dance of the planets, one around the other. In the deepest reality, nature uses that round shape and circle movement to create everything.

The electron goes around the nucleus of the atom. We go travelling around the planet. The planet is rotating around the Sun in our solar system, and our solar system is moving around the universe…, everything in the universe, in essence, is moving in this way. It is a natural movement selected by nature to evolve, and this is the way we move in the Salsa wheel and dancing Salsa in general.

A woman's egg is roundly shaped, also the man's spermatozoid, and once they join to form a baby they still conserve that shape, and in that shape the baby continues growing in the mother's womb, until it is time to give birth. Nature conserves this shape during this process, to make sure, that every part of the living being is well fed, and having this shape during that process, guarantee that if the heart, and the umbilical cord, are in the middle of the body, then, there is an equal distance for the food, and the blood, to be carried to each part of the body, to guarantee the evolution of the living being.

A drop of water, when it is falling to the ground, and whilst in space, will have a roundly shape, which is the same shape, of the planets, because they are also in space. In a way, we can say that in the moment of freedom of contact without anything to be attached to, they are completely free.

We can resume by saying that, in Salsa dance, the wheel, is a representation of the constant creation and evolution in unity and harmony of the Spirit of the human being.

Part 2

The Seven Spiritual Steps Of Dancing Salsa

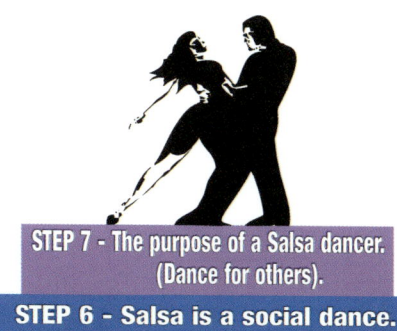

STEP 7 - The purpose of a Salsa dancer. (Dance for others).

STEP 6 - Salsa is a social dance. (Ask for a dance).

STEP 5 - The Rhythm. (All together).

STEP 4 - The emotions of the dancer. (Dance happy).

STEP 3 - The Spirit. (The real dancer).

STEP 2 - The body of the dancer. (The dance partner of your Spirit).

STEP 1 - The mind of the dancer. (Mind your mind).

Figure 10. The Seven Spiritual Steps Of Dancing Salsa.

Chapter 10

STEP 1
The mind of the dancer
(Mind your mind)

STEP 1
The mind of the dancer. (Mind your mind)

Our mind is the biggest treasure given to us by God. It can make us walk, can make us run, or can make us dance with the universe.
Alex Sosa.

There is not a difficult dance, all the knowledge that you will ever need is inside you, you just need to get in contact with it or someone to remind you of that knowledge. All pure knowledge comes from the Spirit, and you also came from the Spirit, and you still are and always will be that Spirit.

The first spiritual step of dancing salsa is to mind your mind, in other words. You need to be conscious that you are conscious, and to be aware of the kind of thoughts your mind is producing at any time. This is a basic principle for us as human beings. This principle is the one that makes us be ahead in God's creation. This is what makes the difference between human beings and the animal Kingdom. When we say to someone *(Think about it)* what we really mean is, take your time, analyze; use your mind.

The mind is the activity of the brain, our centre of command. It is the place where we form and hold our thoughts and ideas. It is the place where we take the decisions that the physical body will execute later. It is the tool that controls the body. Our body is the hardware, and the mind is our software, whatever your mind decides to do, or wherever your mind decides to go, your body, as the mind's tool, will do or follow, for some good reasons your brain is completely protected by bones, and surround for your five senses to experience the outside world, and to grow in the process.

See yourself as a dancer, and keep walking toward that vision.

At the beginning of any learning process, it is very important, to know the reasons for which you want to spend some time, energy and money learning something new, especially to learn how to dance. Some people have very low self-esteem and if the reason that they hold in their minds is not strong enough, they will quit very early. Learning to dance, means to be in front of other people watching you doing different movements that could make you feel uncomfortable if it is your first time, especially, if it is a type of dance that you may find difficult to learn. But you must understand that we all have a beginning, until we master with hard work and practice anything that we

STEP 1
The mind of the dancer. (Mind your mind)

want to achieve.

Everything happens for a reason.

Here I have listed some reasons for why many people consider Salsa music and dance very good for the human being in general (Mind, Body).

For the Mind:
1. Keep your mind active: In Salsa dance you always find new moves and new turns that you will want to learn and this will motivate you, keeping your mind inspired and active, there is always a new challenge.

2. You meet new people: Salsa dance is a very social dance, which means that you will meet new people all the time and in different places; this is a very good opportunity to make new friends and even for business, although we may just go for fun.

3. Make you happy: Salsa music and dance will change your state, and even your life, music and dance are spiritual activities, and this means that they have the capacity to make you feel in a different state of consciousness. In other words, Salsa music and dance will make you feel happy changing your state from a lower to higher one, even watching others dancing and listening to the music will make you feel happy, and happiness is the highest level of spirituality.

For the Body:
1. Keep your body active: Salsa dancing is a high-energy consuming dance. You are in constant movement, and constantly must be aware of what is going on, because of the amount of turns that you will find in this dance. Which means that you will have your entire body in action all the time, and this will help you to keep your health in good conditions, and your body fit.

2. Human body contact: In Salsa dance, you are always in contact with human bodies and hands, and this is a very important action for human beings to take because through our hands we express and communicate ourselves in a good proportion our emotions and feelings, and this hands communication in the dance moment contributes to our relationships as

STEP 1
The mind of the dancer. (Mind your mind)

human beings, and also in our spiritual growth.

3. Breathing becomes deeper: While dancing, you will have no choice but to breathe deeply, Salsa dancing will demand your blood to circulate faster, carrying Oxygen to every part of your body, which will make you breath deeply, bringing good health and revitalizing your body.

There are even, universal reasons, for which we like Salsa music and dance, like for instance:

Bring unity and love to our planet: Salsa music and dance are bringing unity, love and a sense of been in a big family to humanity, and a very good example of this, is the very own history and existence of this music and dance, and today keeps evolving and uniting people all over the planet.

There are even reasons that you may find for yourself, because like in anything else, we all have our own reasons for which we do what we do.

Once we decide the reasons for which we want to start the beautiful process of learning to dance, we must hold these reasons in our mind. Write them down on a piece of paper, and put them in a place where you can see them regularly. This will remind you of the decision you took, and will keep you motivated *(Taking action)*, and inspired *(In Spirit)*.

Your brain is the 5% of your body and takes 20% of your energy. Eat healthy.

Your reasons will be your intention, and your intention is what your mind needs to realize your dreams, your mind will focus on that intention to travel there taking your body as a passenger. Your mind is the most powerful tool in the universe, in fact. The material universe is like a big brain where all the activity happening inside is like a big mind in action, and we are part of this massive mind.

If your mind holds your intention strong and long enough that you get convinced that this is what you really want, then, the universal mind will pick up your signal, and will synchronize everything around you to make sure that you materialize your dreams, becoming a physical reality. Because

STEP 1
The mind of the dancer. (Mind your mind)

that is the reason we were given the mind in the first place, to co-create, to experience joy, and to become our best.

If you look around, you will see that everything was first held in someone else's mind as an idea, and later materialized in the physical reality, for instance, this book you are reading was first an idea in my mind that became a reality with the help of the universal mind, which put the right people and resources in action to make it possible for you to read it, in the same way everything is first an idea, and an idea is a form of energy which has a vibration, and when it is sent out of your mind, will attract similar energy to you, and when you go through life focused on your intention, this powerful energy of your mind is interacting with the rest of the universal energy, like in a big synchronized dance, and is then when you start meeting new people, and be in situations that will help you to materialize your dreams into your reality; because it will be part of their reality also. It will be a mental dance.

Like attract like.

For instance, imagine your mind is a musical instrument like a guitar, and your thoughts are like musical notes. Every time you think about something you are playing a musical note with your mind, and the kind of musical note that you play with your mind will attract this kind of people and experiences into your life. You are building your reality with your mental music *(your thoughts)*. Then, you should play with your mind the music that you really want, and begin to dance happily with your new reality. Only you can make it happen.

Figure 11. Your mental music *(your thoughts)*.

STEP 1
The mind of the dancer. (Mind your mind)

Once you have started the learning process, you must take yourself as your reference point and not other people, you may find people that can say (*Salsa dance is a very difficult dance for you!*) or can say (*You have two left feet!*) Or any kind of negative expressions, and if you pay attention to them they will make weak your intention, will create doubts in your mind, these people are outside you. Only you will have a desire for your intention to be reached.

When a person says something to you, is a reflection of their feelings, of their inside, we all reflex outside how we are feeling inside, how we see ourselves. To give a real opinion to someone, you have to feel like that person. You must be inside that person, and that is something no one can do better than you.

Only you can walk your path. Only you can bring yourself up or down using your mind.

Fearful thoughts will make you feel emotionally weak, and this depletes your immune system, and finally will affect your health. However, you can replace fearful thoughts by happy ones, or positive ones, and your brain will secrete endorphin *(**'The happy hormones'**)* and these hormones, are the ones that make you healthier. You have the free will to pass and keep your mind to the light side, to the positive polarity, and in that way remain working to achieve your dream.

To dance Salsa happily with your body you have to start by dancing happily with your mind.

STEP 1
The mind of the dancer. (Mind your mind)

How to apply the Step 1.

- I will have clear in my mind the reasons why I want to spend some time, energy, and money, learning something new. Especially, to learn how to dance.

- Once I decide the reasons for which I want to start the beautiful process of learning how to dance, I will write these reasons down on a piece of paper, and I will place it where I can see them regularly. This will remind me of the decision I took and keep me motivated, (taking action, moving toward my goal) and keep me inspired (in Spirit).

- I will take control of my mind. I will be aware of my thoughts at all times, knowing that positive thoughts will produce positive actions and as a consequence will bring me closer to reach my goal and this will bring me happiness.

- I will take myself as the reference point and not other people around me that may make my intention weak.

- I will see myself as a Salsa dancer, and remember that the caterpillar will become a butterfly.

Chapter 11

STEP 2
The body of the dancer
(The dance partner of you Spirit)

STEP 2
The body of the dancer (The dance partner of your Spirit).

Like a painter with his brush, a dancer paints the music with the movement of his body.
Alex Sosa

The second spiritual step for dancing Salsa is to be conscious that your body is the dance partner of your Spirit. Your body is the tool for which the Spirit can have a physical experience. They become one when the music stars, in the same way that a painter uses his brush as a tool to express himself and with his tools, he paints his feelings and thoughts, in the same way a dancer uses the body to express himself on the dance floor and in the air, the floor and the air are the canvas where the dancer can paint the music with the movement of his body.

The body is formed by the four elements of nature, Water, Air, Earth, and Fire. These four elements are always in constant movement interaction and transformation, like in an eternal dance. You can see this interaction in nature, in the movement of the current in the river and the sea. The water gets hit by the fire *(Sun)* and becomes rain. The rain falls and feeds the earth bringing life to it. We can see how the volcanoes erupt, and earthquakes move under to change the ground. We have the air element that has its current also, and hurricanes and Typhoons are known for their strong winds. All these four elements are manifested in our bodies. This is what our body is.

For instance, your body is mainly made of water, like our planet earth; your breath that keeps you alive is the air element, the fire element in your body is your emotions *(E-motion: Energy in movement)*, that is why when we have emotional problems our body suffers and changes producing health problems when there is not harmony in them like the harmony in the music.

The four elements in your body:

Water: When you are dancing your body is making a great physical effort, temperature rises and water *(sweat)* come out of the body, a high percentage of your body is made of water, water represents life, every time we dance, we should get the right balance of water in the body to make sure that the body works properly, water is the fuel that keeps the body working properly, water

STEP 2
The body of the dancer (The dance partner of your Spirit).

communicates our whole bodies organs helping them work together to make possible our activities in life, when music communicates with our Spirit, water communicates our bodies, think of water as the music for your body. Your body will be grateful.

Air: Air is another element very important in our body. It carries the Oxygen that our body needs to be alive and to perform properly. Air is another great communicator which we use to communicate between continents, through the air we communicate with each other when we speak, and air is the element that helps to bring the sound of the music to our ears for us to move our bodies when we dance.

Fire: The Fire element in your body are your emotions *(E-MOTIONS), (E)* represents energy and *(MOTIONS)* represents movements. The emotions are a bodily fire to be controlled by us; if not, it can burn us like the fire in the kitchen can burn the house if it gets out of control, emotions are a guiding system given to us to take us in the right direction toward happiness and purpose in life, when we listen to our emotion and not fight with them, we will achieve a great level of understanding of ourselves and this will guide us to a great dancing experience with others.

Earth: The Earth elements in our bodies are the chemical elements that form our body apart from the water, the chemical elements that form our bones, our organs, our arms and legs. It is also our shape; our three-dimensional form. Our body is the recipient who contains all the elements in harmony; our body is the perfect articulated tool on the dance floor for the Spirit to manifest itself creating and experiencing the dance.

Our body is our house, or more importantly it is our real home, because we go to other people houses to visit them but always come back to our own home, the body is our temple it is the home of our real Self, of our spirit. It is the place where we really spend our whole life.

Many people may not be happy with their bodies, and still they feel the attraction to Salsa music to dance. This cannot be an impediment to stop the person interested in dancing Salsa. Our body can be transformed because it is energy and energy can be transformed. I have seen people dancing with

STEP 2
The body of the dancer (The dance partner of your Spirit).

only one leg, also people completely blind dancing. We know about some disc-jockeys who play music for people just using the bass to guide themselves, when the passion for the music gets deep inside you the reaction of your body will be to experience joy. It doesn't matter the external conditions. Go for it.

In our body, we have five methods of perception or physical senses, which are: hearing, sight, touch, smell and taste, these five senses have been given to us to experience reality, to help us to co-create with god, and in god's creation everything must be in harmony, we have been giving also the intellect to create music and play it with our hands, singing and listening to that music with our mouth and ears as a beautiful way to express our feelings, and to dance to that music is another way to express our emotions. In our body, we have all the tools that the Spirit needs to experience happiness on the dance floor. Our body is the car driven by our Spirit. The body gets transformed once the music reaches our ears.

Our body is the tool for which we interact in the three-dimensional reality. It is the tools that allow us to come together making each other happy moving around the dance floor in harmony with the music.

In the same way that we sharp a knife, or learn to ride a bicycle, dedicating time and action *(movement)*, is in this same way that our bodies' movements get better and better practicing on the dance floor.

If we take a moment to look at our body in detail, we will realize how well made our body is and has been designed, how many articulations and joins are taken part of it, everything in proportion to everything else, it is like if the body had been created with the purpose of dancing. The same happens in music, where we find many musical notes and instruments coming together in harmony to create beauty in sound like a symphony, in the same way all our bodies come together in harmony to create the same beauty in movement when we are dancing.

One way to help you to develop your body's awareness is to take a moment each day or a few minutes to just be still and feel the beauty of the creation of your body. It doesn't matter the condition that your body is in. It is a beautiful

STEP 2
The body of the dancer (The dance partner of your Spirit).

master piece of art, take that moment to meditate on your body and think about all the movement that you are intending to do in the future, or maybe you have already learned some turns and movement that you may practice mentally and this mental exercise will bring you awareness about the importance of your body as the dancing partner of your Spirit. This simple exercise will help you a lot in your learning process and in the experience of dancing spiritually.

In a human body, the Spirit has the opportunity to experience the physical reality. The body is the instrument for that experience to happen.

STEP 2
The body of the dancer (The dance partner of your Spirit).

How to apply the Step 2.

- I will be conscious that my body is the dance partner of the Spirit, and is the tool for where the Spirit will enjoy the dance bringing happiness to me and the people around me.

- I will take a moment each day or a few minutes to just be still and feel the beauty of the creation of my body, taking my attention to every part of it, and I will thank my creator for giving me these tools for happiness.

- I will mentally practice some of the turns and movements that I learned during the Salsa classes, and will see myself happy enjoying the dance.

Chapter 12

STEP 3
The Spirit
(The real dancer)

STEP 3
The Spirit. (The real dancer).

Music and dance are the doors to the temple of the human Spirit.
Alex Sosa.

But, What is Spirit?

Spirit : By the Oxford English dictionary:
1. a) **The vital animating essence of a person or animal** (broken in spirit). b) **The soul.**
2. a) **a rational or intelligent being without a material body.** b) a ghost, fairy, etc.
3. **a prevailing mental or moral condition or attitude** (took it in the wrong spirit).
4. (usu.in pl.) esp. Brit. strong distilled liquor, e.g. brandy, whisky, gin, rum.
5. (US esp. in pl.) a) a distilled liquid essence (spirit of turpentine) . b) a distilled alcohol (methylated spirit) . c) a solution of a volatile principle in alcohol (spirit of ammonia).
6. a) **a person's character** (has an unbending spirit) . b) **a person characterized in a specified way** (is an ardent spirit). c) **courage, energy, vivacity** (played with spirit).
7. The real meaning as opposed to lip-service or verbal expression (the spirit of the law). v.tr. (spirited, spiriting) (usu. foll. By away, off, etc.) convey rapidly and secretly by or as if by spirits. In (or in the) spirit sensed psychologically as giving support though not present physically. [from Latin spiritus **'breath, spirit'**].

Spirit: From Wikipedia, the free encyclopedia.
The English word spirit (from Latin spiritus "breath") has many differing meanings and connotations, all of them relating to a non-corporeal substance contrasted with the material body. The spirit of a human being is thus the animating, sensitive or vital principle in that individual, similar to the soul taken to be the seat of the mental, intellectual and emotional powers. The notions of a person's "spirit" and "soul" often also overlap, as both contrast with body and both are imagined as surviving the bodily death in religion and occultism,[1] and "spirit" can also have the sense of "ghost", i.e. manifestations of the spirit of a deceased person.

STEP 3
The Spirit. (The real dancer).

The third spiritual step of dancing Salsa is to realize that you are energy, is to get to know your Spirit. The word Spirit has been used in different ways to describe the essence of a particular thing, inspiration or to be inspired means to be in the Spirit or mood to do something, which implies movement or action *(The Spirit moving the body)*. We also call Spirit to the drinks which, in essence, are based in alcohol. And in a way, what this really means is that, once the alcohol had reached our conscious mind in some degree. We start feeling a litter bit different. In many cultures ancient priests and shamans used to drink some kind of substances to communicate with the Spirits or other form of energy, to bring prosperity to the tribes using this trance as a bridge between dimensions to share information with the gods. They used to dance around a fire, playing some music, and singing songs that make them get into a different state of consciousness, a spiritual level of reality or dimension.

Since the beginnings of mankind; human beings have always searched for God. Some people have different names to identify themselves with this higher force of energy. Many had been looking outside in the material world and others had preferred to look inside the mind. Examples of these are Buddha and Albert Einstein, for instance, while Buddha achieved the light through the mind in meditation, Albert Einstein created the formula $E=M.C^2$, formula that explains that in the material universe, everything is energy and that the matter is energy that it can be transformed if the speed of light in it is changed.

"I want to know God's thoughts ... the rest are details"   Albert Einstein

Other great philosophers like Plato and Socrates, among many other thinkers, studied very closely the effects of the music in the soul of the human beings, and many statements they wrote to guide us in this subject:

"In order to take the spiritual temperature of an individual or society, one must mark the music"   Plato.

All around the world human beings believe in a higher intelligence, a supreme energy that guides and protects us; we pray to this energy. We dance and play music to invite this energy to come to us and manifest its self.

STEP 3
The Spirit. (The real dancer).

To be inspired means to be in the spirit to move and take action toward your goals

Everything in the three-dimensional plane is a manifestation of this higher energy it is what we call the creation, everything that we do with inspiration is just this living force working through our bodies as an instrument to build our reality, a musician feels this energy in his highest moments of creation, and he called muse to this energy. The dancers feel this energy through this music, and the body gets transformed with the sound, exactly like Einstein explained, and the mind controlling the body as Buddha did.

Music and dance are expressions of the Spirit of the human being, when we enjoy dancing we are spiritual and physically vibrating in harmony, and we have our mind, emotions and body in total alignment. This is the moment in which the Spirit can manifest and express itself in total freedom, music and dance in harmony *(Rhythm)* is like a bridge for where once in place the Spirit in us can travel from the unseen world to the three-dimensional plane to enjoy.

Exist a very powerful emotional connection between a musician and his music at the moment of the musical creation, in the same way that exists between the dancer and the feelings that this experiences while dancing to the music, she/he likes. This connection cannot be seen by the human eye, neither can be touched by the hands. This connection can only be perceived and experienced inside our body in a spiritual way through our conciseness.

To dance spiritually means to dance consciously aware of our emotions, of what we are feeling in that very magic moment of the dancing experience, bringing happiness as a result of our higher vibration to others that are dancing with us, is to share this energetic love for the music to our dancing partners and to the observers around us through our bodies' movements.

Today science, religions, and many other forms of beliefs are agreed that everything in the universe is energy or light, matter, and information.

According to scientists the beginning of the universe was the big bang, which means energy in movement. Everything is energy, the photons *(little*

STEP 3
The Spirit. (The real dancer).

points of light or energy) collapse with each other forming proton, neutrons, electrons and maybe other particles, which in various combinations form everything in the physical universe; in other words, everything in the universe is made from light or energy, and the universe is constantly expanding and evolving.

According to religions and other forms of beliefs, the beginning of the universe or creation is light or consciousness *(God)*. Everything is light or consciousness, and consciousness is always expanding in an evolutionary impulse to create and illuminate all beings.

Science:	Religion:
Energy/Light.	GOD/Light/Consciousness.
-No space *(Every where)*.	- Omnipresent.
-No time *(Infinity)*.	- Omnipotent.
-No matter *(Everything/Information)*.	- Omniscient.

Figure 12. In order to make some comparisons here we present some aspects of these two apparently different points of view.

The scientist discovered that the speed of light is 300.000 km/s and at this speed, the physical matter becomes cero, and transforms completely into the light, which means no space, no time, no matter, going back to its original state.

Energy in nature is always evolving and never falls back. It is an eternal impulse to create and to evolve, to be conscious of itself.

Now, what has this to do with Spirit?
To answer this question we must reach to the conclusion that science, religions and the other forms of beliefs are meeting today in a middle point, they are talking about Energy/Light in a similar way, which can only make us accept that this is what we really are, Energy/Light.

Spirit can only be the highest vibration of the Energy or Light, which is the essence of the universe according to science, and according to religion, it is GOD.

STEP 3
The Spirit. (The real dancer).

We are the Spirit materialized, dense, in time and space. We are the other side of the high vibration. We can pass to the highest vibration through two aspects of creation *(sound and movement in harmony)*, music and dance, and when we dance, in that moment of high vibration, we have transformed our body influencing our cells. We are changing our molecules with pure light. We are bringing health and happiness to our body and to the people that are enjoying looking at us in this positive state, we are evolving, we are dancing with the essence of life. In this moment, we feel different because we are experiencing a different state of consciousness, because our nature has changed, our vibration changed, but all of this happens with the help of the mind. The mind is the key to the door of consciousness for the body to go through, in this moment of experience you are mentally pure energy and pure energy is omnipotent, omnipresent and omniscient, in this moment you forget time, space and identity if you really give yourself to the experience, in this moment of happiness you are pure Spirit, pure Light, pure essence and that is the reason for which it feels so good, and that is why when the music stops; We want more of that feeling, of that high state, of that experience. We want to carry on that moment of pure energy and pure happiness.

The Spirit is an impulse to evolve and to create. It is the force of nature; It is the impulse to evolve from lower to higher form of complexity. The dancer merges with the music. Dancer and musician become one, sound and movement in unity and harmony, experiencing infinity. Spirit is the highest vibration of the universal energy, and spirituality is where the past, present and future merge to become eternity.

The Spirit in you is always evolving, always changing. That is the nature of the Spirit, that is the nature of the light inside you; of your essence, and that is the reason for which Salsa music and dance are the result of a great mix between different cultures, and that is the reason why this type of music and dance is so well received in different parts of the world. It is a mix of sounds and movements that have had an impulse to evolve and keep evolving and mixing even today.

That is why when we ask a person what they are feeling when they are dancing, they use expressions like: freedom, happiness, and many other po-

STEP 3
The Spirit. (The real dancer).

sitive expressions, because that is the nature of the Spirit that is the part of you that wants to evolve, and if you let your mind put barriers to your learning process or to your dancing experiences with negativity, false images or bad thoughts, then, all the positive feelings that can be experienced will not happen.

Exist the material reality and the spiritual reality; they are connected with each other. They are two sides of the same coin. We can dance just physically to the music, or we can dance spiritually also. This is just a matter of focus and awareness, knowing what is really happening inside and outside our bodies will help us to grow our perception of our reality and to reach the inter-connectivity of our body with our Spirit.

You have to open the doors of your mind for the Spirit to come forward, bringing your heights potential out to evolve.

Once you know who you really are and what is happening inside and outside of you, then you will be enlightened (in light, in knowledge of), just relax and enjoy the dance with your Spirit.

STEP 3
The Spirit. (The real dancer).
How to apply the Step 3.

-I will meditate and realize that in the universe, everything is energy, and I'm part of the universe, I'm energy.

- I will be conscious that once I have my mind, emotions and body in total alignment, this is the moment in which the Spirit can manifest and express itself in total freedom.

-I will dance consciously aware of my emotions, allowing the Spirit to travel from the unseen world to the three-dimensional plane using the music and dance in harmony, relaxing my body, giving up every muscle of my body to the music to enjoy the dance.

Chapter 13

STEP 4
The emotions
of the dancer
(Dance happy)

STEP 4
The emotions of the dancer. (Dance happy).

Spiritual dancing is not just about moving your body to the music, but also feeling the music with your heart, touching the music with your soul.

Alex Sosa.

The fourth spiritual step of dancing Salsa is your emotions. The word emotion often is interpreted as something bad or some kind of state that we don't really want to be in, and as a result we don't pay too much attention to them; and in many cases, we try to avoid them. We think that we are in control of them all the time if we don't get "emotional," but the truth is that emotions are your best friends, and good friends are always by your side, in good moments you don't have to call them because they know they are always welcome as a part of you, and in bad moments, they always arrive at be by your side to support and advise you, to help you grow. In the same way emotions are your guiding system, emotions have been given to you to help you grow in life, to make you better, to correct your actions, to take you to the next level and finally arrive at your destination to realize your purpose in life. You need to listen to your emotions. They are energy in motion *(E=Energy, Motion=Movement)*, energy talking to you in their own language, which is the language that your Spirit uses to guide you to happiness; to be your best and avoid painful experiences.

"When you oppose resistance, and do not listen to your emotions, you suffer"

Emotions can be manifested in two ways. Negative emotions and positive emotions. Negative emotions arise from negative thinking, and positive emotions arise from positive thinking. In terms of energy, positive emotions are the harmonious illuminated side in each of us. It is the light side, the side that once we are in we experience happiness, joy, love, health, purpose and all the highest vibrations that come from the Spirit which is the force behind these positive emotions. On the other side we have the negative emotions, which are the dark side of ourselves *(The ego)*, the side that does not have light of its own, and once we get into this dark side mentally we do not see with clarity what is really going on outside us physically. Negative emotion blinds us completely, and does not let us grow in our lives if we don't listen to them and correct our actions. In this dark side we experience many negative emotions like frustration, anger, fear, disappointment and more.

STEP 4
The emotions of the dancer. (Dance happy).

It is like if our mind gets into complete darkness and as a consequence everything outside us gets completely dark, and we all know what happens when we are in a dark room, we start knocking things over and losing balance. We get scared of the obscurity, and we do not really want to move forward until we turn on the light.

Many times I have seen Salsa students get very emotional because they find difficulty learning some Salsa steps or some difficult turns. In other cases some students feel very frustrated because they are not learning fast enough or some are not happy with the style they are learning after seeing other styles that they find more interesting and fun. The truth is that there are many reasons for which we as humans can get emotional, many people express their emotions in different ways according to what is happening to them and their personalities, but in every case, the emotions are a guiding system that is telling you to pay attention to whatever you are thinking before you react or take any action. Emotions rise from feelings, feelings rise from thoughts, thoughts are a product of the mind, it is what the mind does and can produce conscious or unconscious, which means that we do have the capacity to dominate or control them if we are aware of them in any moment.

For instance: My Salsa teacher said something to me to correct my moves in front of the rest of the students, and I didn't like it, immediately my mind produced the following thoughts.

- How embarrassing!
- I will not carry on here!
- People may think I'm …!
- This teacher is not good!

All these thoughts are being produced voluntarily. It is something that I'm doing in my mind as an inside reacting consequence of what just happened outside. These are negative thoughts that with some repetition in the mind will take energy and become feelings, and once they become feelings, they will build up more energy until we are ready to fire the reactive emotion *(Negative energy)* to whoever pulls the trigger. These negative thoughts which are the beginning of the reactive emotions can be replaced consciously by us, by our mind. We just have to desire to do it and take that

STEP 4
The emotions of the dancer. (Dance happy).

mental action. This is something not easy to do because this means that we have to be really aware of these thoughts when they arrive and automatically use the positive ones to take us to a different positive emotional-mental state like turning on the light in a dark room, that mental action in return will make us feel better, and as a result we will get the guidance, the meaning and purpose of what is happening outside us and learn the message to grow inside.

Here is an example:

- My Salsa dance teacher said something to me to correct my move in front of the rest of the students, and I didn't like it.

Immediately my mind produced the following thoughts:

Negative thoughts	Replace by: Positive thoughts
1- How embarrassing!	1- He/She cares about my progress, What he/she is trying to tell me?
2- I will not carry on here!	2- I will come here again
3- People may think I'm ...!	3- Others learn with my mistakes/ I learn from their mistakes also.
4- This teacher is bad!	4- This teacher is very good.

Figure 13. Negative thoughts / Replace by Positive thoughts.

This does not means that you have to let people treat you badly, we all know when someone is not behaving correctly, but, certainly, negative emotions are never the permanent solution to our problems, and instead they are a call to change, to pay attention to the road and turn in the right direction to reach the destination.

Your positive emotions are an indicator that you are going in the right direction towards your destination. Your negative emotions are an indicator that you are going backward in the opposite side, going far from where you supposed to be. Pay attention to them and put yourself in the right direction.

STEP 4
The emotions of the dancer. (Dance happy).

How to apply the Step 4.

- I will pay attention to whatever I'm thinking before I react or take any action, aware that my thoughts are the beginning of my emotions.

- I will listen to my emotions. They are energy in motion (E=Energy, Motion=Movement), energy talking to me in their own language, which is the language that my Spirit uses to guide me to happiness; to be my best and to avoid in that way painful experiences.

- I will keep a positive attitude at all times during my Salsa dance learning process.

Chapter 14

STEP 5
The Rhythm
(All together)

STEP 5
The Rhythm. (All together)

Music is the spiritual evolution of sound. Dance is the spiritual evolution of movement, and rhythm is the harmony between the Spirit and the human body in the eternal dance of creation.
Alex Sosa.

Rhythm: By the Oxford English dictionary.
1. a measured flow of words and phrases in verse or prose determined by the length of and stress on syllables.
2. a) the aspect of musical composition concerned with periodical accent and the duration of notes. b) a particular type of pattern formed by this (samba rhythm).
3. physiol. Movement with a regular succession of strong and weak elements.
4. a regular recurring pattern of events or actions. [from Greek rhuthmos]. Rhythmless adj.

Rhythm: From Wikipedia, the free encyclopedia.
Rhythm, a sequence in time repeated, featured in dance: an early moving picture demonstrates the waltz.
Simple [quadr]duple drum pattern, against which duration is measured in much popular music: divides two beats into two Play (help·info).
Compound triple drum pattern: divides three beats into three. Play (help·info) Contains repetition on three levels. For other uses, see Rhythm (disambiguation).
Rhythm (from Greek ῥυθμός rhythmos, "any regular recurring motion, symmetry"[1]) may be generally defined as a "movement marked by the regulated succession of strong and weak elements, or of opposite or different conditions." [2] This general meaning of regular recurrence or pattern in time may be applied to a wide variety of cyclical natural phenomena having a periodicity or frequency of anything from microseconds to millions of years.

The fifth spiritual step for dancing Salsa is the Rhythm. Rhythm is to move your body in harmony and in the mathematical right time with the music. Rhythm is the intelligent capacity of the universe to synchronize everything with everything else with harmony and love, knowing the right time for each season, keeping life manifesting and renewing itself in an eternal circle. It is

STEP 5
The Rhythm. (All together)

like if the word universe *(One verse)* is the music and everything that exists in it were dancing with everything else in an eternal dance.

If we look at a tree in the winter when it is windy, we will see how the tree moves in harmony with the wind, if the wind doesn't blow the tree will not move, if the wind blows stronger the tree responds with more movements, and even the leafs will produce sounds like music being played in harmony with the movement of the tree. The same happens with the sea and the waves, with our heart and our mind. Stronger emotions produced as a result of our thoughts will accelerate our heart beats, and if we listen to our heart, we can hear the beats increasing accordingly with our emotions. Everything has a rhythm in nature. Rhythm is the mathematical tool of the spirit to be manifest creatively in our physical reality through sound and movement in harmony.

For instance, for a word to come out of our mouth there have to be a connection between the mind, the vocal cords and the mouth, and with this coordination, when it is in place we can express our ideas through sound, this is rhythm between our body, and the same happens with the mind, body and Spirit on the dance floor with the music playing, everything coming together in alignment and rhythm in an expression of happiness and joy.

First do not worry about your body movements and let the music take you, you have to concentrate yourself in the music, and your body will gradually move following the music, remember that sound transforms matter.

Time is Gold.

For instance, if you arrive late to a meeting you lose business. A mother has to wait nine months to see and hold her baby in her arms. In Salsa dance, we have to respect the rhythm *(The Clave pattern)*. You must have harmony between the music and the body, They have to be one, your body and the music have to hold each other tie and keep together in harmony. Look at the rhythm in nature everything is happening at the right time looking for balance and harmony. In Salsa dance we must do the same, there is a right time for every step, and it is the music who guides our bodies through that journey.

STEP 5
The Rhythm. (All together)

First, you get the timing of the rhythm in the music (The Clave pattern), then you add the movements of your body in harmony to it, and let the spirit in you take over. The same thing you find in nature, everything in nature is moving according to a sound and in harmony with it, and as a result creation is manifested to carry on the evolution.

STEP 5
The Rhythm. (All together)

How to apply the Step 5.

- I will not worry about my body's movements and will first let the music take me; I will concentrate myself in the music and let my body gradually move with rhythm.

- I will respect the rhythm *(The Clave pattern)*. I must have harmony between the music and the body; they have to be one.

- I will look how everything in nature is moving according to a sound and in harmony to that sound and that will help me to dance in Clave.

Chapter 15

STEP 6
Salsa is
a social dance
(Ask for a dance)

STEP 6
Salsa is a social dance. (Ask for a dance)

When you ask for a dance, you are giving a dance.
Alex Sosa.

The sixth spiritual step of dancing Salsa is the understanding that Salsa is a social dance. Human beings are social creatures. We need to socialize to evolve, and Salsa is a Social dance. It is a dance which demands communication between the dancers on the dance floor. It needs eye and body contact, also spiritual contact with the music to enjoy it in the highest level. If we look at the history of the Salsa dance, like many other types of dance like Rumba, Guaguanco, etc, we will discover that these are dances created in poor places economically speaking, but it is in these circumstances that the human being seems to go inside to look for something to balance the outside and is when we get in contact with our inner self, it is when we get in contact with the light inside us, with our Spirit. In poor material circumstance humans beings need to share to survive, and it is in these places and circumstance when the Spirit likes to manifest itself free from the egoistic concepts of the mind and bring out spiritual creations, like music and dance, nothing that lives alone can survive, for instance, our body's organs are all working together to keep us alive. Every organ is working for the whole, for the benefit of every other organ. Every cell of the body is doing the same, but the minute a cell becomes selfish and starts taking just for itself it becomes a cancer.

Salsa dance is about sharing happiness with others in a social way, and expressing yourself through your body's movements.

Dancing with others means that others will dance with you, this may look like a very obvious statement but in many cases we go to dance Salsa and we wait for someone to ask us for a dance, we feel a bit uncomfortable to ask for many reasons, and we list some of them to see if you identify yourself with any of these situations.

1. I'm a shy person, I prefer to wait for someone to ask me for a dance.
2. I'm a beginner, I prefer to dance just with beginners.
3. I'm not good, and need to improve before I ask.
4. I'm good, and only dance with good dancers.

STEP 6
Salsa is a social dance. (Ask for a dance)

In all these situations the motivation is the same. We want to feel good. We do not want to put ourselves in difficult situations, but in doing this we are stopping ourselves from many experiences, for instance:

If you feel you are a shy person, and you let that image of yourself stop you from asking someone for a dance; then you may spend the whole night without a dance, and it could happen that someone next to you may be thinking exactly the same, in the end, we go to Salsa places to dance and have fun.

If you are a beginner, perhaps you should consider that your best way to grow is experiencing dancing, your experiences are with someone who already knows what you need to learn, and believe me, many people will be happy to help you if you ask, is our real nature as human beings; and in reality, when we decide to learn a dance we are spiritually growing. Dancing, like playing a musical instrument is a very spiritual activity, and this means that you will be sensitive enough to help someone else if they need help. And if you want to dance, and you are a beginner, then you have many people around you ready to help you, just ask and will be given.

If you think you are not good, **and you need to improve before asking someone for a dance**, you should perhaps consider, that like everything else in life, to learn to dance Salsa is not about a destination, it is the journey that you will really enjoy. There is always something new to learn, and new creations always come to light. And after all, the best way to learn is by practicing.

If you think you are very good, and only dance with good dancers, you are cutting yourself from the beautiful experience of teaching and helping others, and the more you teach the more you learn, you never know who can give you an idea to create a new move, many good ideas have come from mistakes and in the five steps of learning, which are: Silence, listen, practice, understand and teach, clearly once you know something, the best way to keep it with you is giving it to someone else because the more you teach the more you practice what you know. Knowledge is like happiness, is something that grows when is shared with more people, helping others is helping yourself.

STEP 6
Salsa is a social dance. (Ask for a dance)

Then we should go to Salsa places to enjoy this social dance, sharing happiness, to help if someone needs it and to learn as a consequence.

We need culture to develop. Many of our values come from culture. The self does not evolve in isolation. It needs culture to evolve and Salsa music and dance are the result of all these cultures mixed through many years of interaction.

In Salsa places you can meet people from different walks of life; you may meet business people or the person that can be your partner for the rest of your life.

The reality is that salsa dance is a social dance, and it is a natural and easy way to get in contact with people and to make different relationships. It is like a big family gathering together to spend some time in happiness.

STEP 6
Salsa is a social dance. (Ask for a dance)

How to apply the Step 6.

- I will go to Salsa places to enjoy this social dance, sharing happiness.

-I will ask people for a dance, knowing that they are waiting to dance with me.

- I will help anyone who may need my help, and teach what I know, this will make someone happy and will give happiness back to me, and I will learn as a consequence.

Chapter 16

STEP 7
The purpose of a Salsa dancer
(Dance for others)

STEP 7
The Salsa dancer purpose. (Dance for others)

Dance for yourself and you will change a life, dance for others, and you will change the planet.

Alex Sosa.

The seventh spiritual step of dancing Salsa is your purpose as a Salsa dancer. We all have a purpose in life. We all have something to offer to someone else. If your purpose is to become a good Salsa dancer to teach other people to dance, and in that way they can experience the same things you do, then, you should make it happen, and this will bring you happiness, if you just learn because you are attracted to the vibrations of this music, and you feel happy dancing Salsa, any way you will bring happiness to the people that will dance with you.

Information helps us change. Experience makes us grow.

Everything that you learn about Salsa dance only has meaning when you enjoy in a spiritual dance, when you see the happiness in the face of others dancing with you.

To be a Salsa dancer	=	Intention Attention Purpose	+	Learn Practice Teach

Figure 14. *To be a Salsa dancer.*

Once you receive the call of your Spirit, telling you that it feels attracted to the Salsa music vibrations, and to the movements of this dance, then you should follow it, this is a call for freedom, this is a call to happiness, to spiritual expression. This is a process that once begun should not be abandoned. We are all learning, and it is this process which guides us in our purpose in life.

When you dance for others you become the song played, your movements will be creating satisfaction to you and to the person dancing with you, will be a spiritual dance, you will be dancing with your Spirit.

STEP 7
The Salsa dancer purpose. (Dance for others)

All that you have learned and all your experiences as a Salsa dancer can be shared and practiced with everyone else, and in this way you will make many people happy, and in that moment, you will understand that everything you went through to become a Salsa dancer has been worthwhile, that is the reason and the purpose of a Salsa dancer.

You have come here to dance with life. Life is always changing, transforming, vibrating. This is what nature does and this is the reality.

Everything came from the Spirit, from infinity, from the Light, and all we see in our world is a consequence of what happens at that level, if we want to become a Salsa dancer and make our life happier and the life of many people, we just have to desire it as our purpose, and by seeing everything as if it is already happening, we are on the way to reach it.

In order to achieve our purpose as a Salsa dancer we should start by looking at the end of the journey, because in the process of learning we can't understand our purpose in the middle. Every purpose reveals itself at the right time, and this always happens at the final stage of any learning process, and clearly, there is not action without purpose and only people that don't know why and where they are going can reach nowhere.

Don't let other people to take away your purpose once you have decided it, only you know where you want to go, and just you will find the way to get there.

When we are connected with each other spiritually in a dance, we are in that moment connected to the Spirit, to God, to the highest energy vibration, to the Light inside us.

You are the vehicle through which the Spirit can express and share love and happiness with the rest of humanity. If you decide to learn to dance Salsa to teach others, and in that way you will be sharing happiness and love as your purpose in life, then, you can rest with the guaranty that this is what you will receive also from the people you help. If you become a cable for that energy to pass trough you, then, you will give and receive the same energy. When we are connected to our purpose we are happy people, because we are

STEP 7
The Salsa dancer purpose. (Dance for others)

in the universe, everything is working together to survive and evolve, taking what we need and giving what we can for the well-being of the whole. This is something that happens in the macrocosms between galaxies, in our planet between the ecosystem; and also in the micro world with the atoms; even in our bodies we can see this cooperation between the organs working hard to keep us alive. This cooperation can only not be found in the mind of an egoistic person. Only pure love can make that cooperation that produces life possible.

Love your neighbour as yourself.

When you have the purpose of dancing for others, to see them happy, you are dancing with love, then the well-being of others is felt as your own because at the deepest level you and the person that is dancing with you are made from the same energy, you are two parts of a big family, and that is the true nature of humanity, that is the nature of the creator, and that is the meaning of what we call dancing with your Spirit. That is the purpose of a Salsa dancer.

STEP 7
The Salsa dancer purpose. (Dance for others)

How to apply the Step 7.

- When I dance Salsa, I will keep in mind that I'm giving happiness to the person dancing with me and to the people that may be watching the dance.

- My purpose can be to teach other people to dance and in doing so I'm bringing more people to my experiences, and also sharing love and happiness with the rest of the planet.

Conclusion

Conclusion

The human being and the whole of nature is supposed to be connected. Nothing in nature can exist in isolation. When an amount of water gets separated from the river, and does not have any contact with anything else, it becomes green and smelly, and ultimately will dry out. We are part of a big river of energy, and we need to be and feel that connection between us. In the quantum level particles' exchange energy, and in this way they interact with each other. In the same way we exchange energy on the dance floor dancing with each other in the wheel or in partners. And the musicians playing their music for us to enjoy dancing, knowing that our happiness becomes their happiness also, the more we enjoy; the more happiness they experience. In the animal Kingdom we see how they depend on food to survive physically, they live in the present, and desire according to their needs, but, human beings need that level of surviving and another level more important than the physical level, human beings need to ask the big questions: *Who am I?, Why I'm here?, Where I'm going?, What is this all about?*. And that is the difference from the animals. We need to live purposely. We need to survive spiritually. We supposed to be the more evolved ones for a reason, and that reason is love, harmony, peace, and the power to realize that at the deepest level we are one, and inside us, at the quantum level, we are something that cannot be separated without losing significance, meaning, or purpose. We are part of a purposely evolution, that as far as our mind can grasp is happening for a reason, that reason can become many if we feel like we are separated beings, and one, if we live in peace, sharing love and harmony in the whole planet, like we do in Salsa music and dance when we are in a big Salsa party, or in a Salsa club, where we are all sharing the same oxygen, the same music, and dancing with people that we meet in many cases for the first time in our life. And even so, we give them happiness whilst dancing, and we receive that happiness back from them at the same time.

In Salsa music and dance we are applying the principle of giving and receiving all the time. We can apply this principle to our whole life and make this planet a huge Salsa party, and the universe can have the humanity of this planet completely unified physically and spiritually at the end. That will always be a new beginning.

Applying all the steps

Step 1. The mind of the dancer. *(Mind your mind).*

- I will have clear in my mind the reasons why I want to spend some time, energy, and money, learning something new. Especially, to learn how to dance.

- Once I decide the reasons for which I want to start the beautiful process of learning how to dance, I will write these reasons down on a piece of paper, and I will place it where I can see them regularly. This will remind me of the decision I took and keep me motivated, (taking action, moving toward my goal) and keep me inspired (in Spirit).

- I will take control of my mind. I will be aware of my thoughts at all times, knowing that positive thoughts will produce positive actions and as a consequence will bring me closer to reach my goal and this will bring me happiness.

- I will take myself as the reference point and not other people around me that may make my intention weak.

- I will see myself as a Salsa dancer, and remember that the caterpillar will become a butterfly.

Step 2. The body of the dancer. *(The dance partner of your Spirit).*

- I will be conscious that my body is the dance partner of the Spirit, and is the tool for where the Spirit will enjoy the dance bringing happiness to me and the people around me.

- I will take a moment each day or a few minutes to just be still and feel the beauty of the creation of my body, taking my attention to every part of it, and I will thank my creator for giving me these tools for happiness.

- I will mentally practice some of the turns and movements that I learned during the Salsa classes, and will see myself happy enjoying the dance.

Applying all the steps

Step 3. The spirit. *(The real dancer).*

-I will meditate and realize that in the universe, everything is energy, and I'm part of the universe, I'm energy.

- I will be conscious that once I have my mind, emotions and body in total alignment, this is the moment in which the Spirit can manifest and express itself in total freedom.

-I will dance consciously aware of my emotions, allowing the Spirit to travel from the unseen world to the three-dimensional plane using the music and dance in harmony, relaxing my body, giving up every muscle of my body to the music to enjoy the dance.

Step 4. The dancer's emotions. *(Dance happy).*

- I will pay attention to whatever I'm thinking before I react or take any action, aware that my thoughts are the beginning of my emotions.

- I will listen to my emotions. They are energy in motion (E=Energy, Motion=Movement), energy talking to me in their own language, which is the language that my Spirit uses to guide me to happiness; to be my best and to avoid in that way painful experiences.

- I will keep a positive attitude at all times during my Salsa dance learning process.

Step 5. The Rhythm. *(All together).*

- I will not worry about my body's movements and will first let the music take me; I will concentrate myself in the music and let my body gradually move with rhythm.

- I will respect the rhythm *(The Clave pattern)*. I must have harmony between the music and the body; they have to be one.

- I will look how everything in nature is moving according to a sound and in

Applying all the steps

harmony to that sound and that will help me to dance in Clave.

Step 6. Salsa is a social dance. *(Ask for a dance).*

- I will go to Salsa places to enjoy this social dance, sharing happiness.

-I will ask people for a dance, knowing that they are waiting to dance with me.

- I will help anyone who may need my help, and teach what I know, this will make someone happy and will give happiness back to me, and I will learn as a consequence.

Step 7. The purpose of a Salsa dancer. *(Dance for others).*

- When I dance Salsa, I will keep in mind that I'm giving happiness to the person dancing with me and to the people that may be watching the dance.

- My purpose can be to teach other people to dance and in doing so I'm bringing more people to my experiences, and also sharing love and happiness with the rest of the planet.

Why Salsa?.

Here I present to you some of the answers given by some Salsa dancers in a survey done by me some years ago on internet and in some Salsa clubs in UK, you can see in these answers how they explain their emotions in their peak moment of satisfaction of the dancing experience, and also other points about Salsa music and dance in general.

The survey was titled, **Why Salsa?**

Dancer 1:
1. **When did you start to dance Salsa?:**
'A year ago'
2. **What interested you to dance Salsa?:**
'Love of dancing.........& men!'
3. **How do you feel while dancing Salsa?:**
'Happy, confident & sexy'
4. **your partner dance Salsa? if not, why?:**
'No partner :-('
5. **Your experience while dancing La Rueda?:**
'Good fun & mentally stimulating'
6. **What style do you prefer? Why?:**
'Cuban style because of its freer moves'
7. **Any favourite Salsa Song?:**
'So many good ones to mention'
8. **Any other Comment?**
'Love it!"

Dancer 2:
1. **When did you start to dance Salsa?:**
'2001'
2. **What interested you to dance Salsa?:**
'social live, relax'
3. **How do you feel while dancing Salsa?:**
'super'
4. **your partner dance Salsa? if not, why?:**
'yes'
5. **Your experience while dancing La Rueda?:**
'great'
6. **What style do you prefer? Why?:**
'cuban'
7. **Any favourite Salsa Song?:**
'songs from charanga habanera'
8. **Any other Comment?**

Why Salsa?.

Dancer 3:
1. **When did you start to dance Salsa?:**
'6 years ago'
2. **What interested you to dance Salsa?:**
'socialising, new dance and having fun'
3. **How do you feel while dancing Salsa?:**
'invigorated'
4. **your partner dance Salsa? if not, why?:**
'yes'
5. **Your experience while dancing La Rueda?:**
'excellent and engaging, family like!'
6. **What style do you prefer? Why?:**
'Cuban'
7. **Any favourite Salsa Song?:**
'Esperanza Calle Real'
8. **Any other Comment?**
'london needs more cuban places to eat and socialise.'

Dancer 4:
1. **When did you start to dance Salsa?:**
'August/September 2006'
2. **What interested you to dance Salsa?:**
'I like dancing, and salsa looks fun.'
3. **How do you feel while dancing Salsa?:**
'I enjoy it.'
4. **your partner dance Salsa? if not, why?:**
'No, he dances other styles.'
5. **Your experience while dancing La Rueda?:**
'I do not do rueda.'
6. **What style do you prefer? Why?:**
'On 1, because as far as I am concerned, it fits the music better.'
7. **Any favourite Salsa Song?:**
''
8. **Any other Comment?**
'Music played in salsa clubs is getting faster, which in my opinion, is damaging to the quality of the dance and to the dancers' enjoyment.'

Dancer 5:
1. **When did you start to dance Salsa?:**
'In cuba en i was a child'
2. **What interested you to dance Salsa?:**
'I am a cuban'
3. **How do you feel while dancing Salsa?:**
'It make me feel happy and full of energy'

Why Salsa?.

4. your partner dance Salsa? if not, why?:
'Yes'
5. Your experience while dancing La Rueda?:
'learning more steps'
6. What style do you prefer? Why?:
'Cuban because more enjoyable'
7. Any favourite Salsa Song?:
'Y que tu quiere que te den. Adalberto y su son'
8. Any other Comment?
''

Dancer 6:
1. When did you start to dance Salsa?:
'April 2007'
2. What interested you to dance Salsa?:
'Music, exercise and to meet people'
3. How do you feel while dancing Salsa?:
'Wonderful'
4. your partner dance Salsa? if not, why?:
'No partner'
5. Your experience while dancing La Rueda?:
'Great fun'
6. What style do you prefer? Why?:
'Cuban, just like the feel of it'
7. Any favourite Salsa Song?:
"
8. Any other Comment?
''

Dancer 7:
1. When did you start to dance Salsa?:
'2002'
2. What interested you to dance Salsa?:
'I just love the music and dancing to it is great'
3. How do you feel while dancing Salsa?:
'With a good partner, as if I am flying or floating depending on the type of music'
4. your partner dance Salsa? if not, why?:
'Some times'
5. Your experience while dancing La Rueda?:
"
6. What style do you prefer? Why?:
'anything with pace'
7. Any favourite Salsa Song?:
''

~123~

Why Salsa?.

Dancer 8:
1. **When did you start to dance Salsa?:**
'In the late 1980's'
2. **What interested you to dance Salsa?:**
'You can get away with being shy'
3. **How do you feel while dancing Salsa?:**
'Sometimes Contained and sometimes just expressively free.'
4. **your partner dance Salsa? if not, why?:**
'Yes.'
5. **Your experience while dancing La Rueda?:**
'Not to keen on it.'
6. **What style do you prefer? Why?:**
'Cuban Folkloric. Combining all the original roots into dance.'
7. **Any favourite Salsa Song?:**
'no'
8. **Any other Comment?**
'

Dancer 9:
1. **When did you start to dance Salsa?:**
'2002'
2. **What interested you to dance Salsa?:**
'Active, social.'
3. **How do you feel while dancing Salsa?:**
'Amazing, revitalised!'
4. **your partner dance Salsa? if not, why?:**
'No, back problems.'
5. **Your experience while dancing La Rueda?:**
'good fun'
6. **What style do you prefer? Why?:**
'Cuban'
7. **Any favourite Salsa Song?:**
'Anything Cuban'
8. **Any other Comment?**
'Why is there so little Cuban dancing, and so much cross body?'

Why Salsa?.

Dancer 10:
1. When did you start to dance Salsa?:
'I tried lessons firstly about 5 years ago but only went to 3'
2. What interested you to dance Salsa?:
'My love of dancing in general, especially fast dancing (as opposed to ballrooom), plus I love a challenge and to learn it was a challenge for me. I also loved watching people dance salsa and longed to try it. It is also a social thing where you meet new people and make friends and well as keeping fit.'
3. Experience while dancing Salsa?:
''
4. your partner dance Salsa? if not, why?:
'No, although he did go to a few lessons a couple of years ago. He is generally lazy and can't be bothered to go now.'
5. Your experience while dancing La Rueda?:
'have only tried it a few times, found it a bit tricky at first but then picked it up'
6. What style do you prefer? Why?:
'cross body as I find it more interesting, cuban is too easy now'
7. Any favourite Salsa Song?:
'no'
8. Any other Comment?

Dancer 11:
1. When did you start to dance Salsa?:
'Feb 2004'
2. What interested you to dance Salsa?:
'It never a friend wanted to try it so I just followed'
3. Experience while dancing Salsa?:
'??'
4. your partner dance Salsa? if not, why?:
'Yes'
5. Your experience while dancing La Rueda?:
'Dont like it cause people take it took serious and forget to have fun'
6. What style do you prefer? Why?:
'Cuban as its not so spin city'
7. Any favourite Salsa Song?:
'No'
8. Any other Comment?:
'Music gets boring after a while cause were ever you go the tracks are the same. Im hearing the same tracks from when I first started'

Dancer 12:
1. When did you start to dance Salsa?:
'7 years ago'
2. What interested you to dance Salsa?:
'the fun element'

Why Salsa?.

3. Experience while dancing Salsa?:
'Love it! '
4. your partner dance Salsa? if not, why?:
'No, not interested'
5. Your experience while dancing La Rueda?:
'Fabulous especially if you get the right teacher that makes it fun and exciting. '
6. What style do you prefer? Why?:
'La rueda and casino, salsa is salsa. It must be Cuban salsa however, none of that NY style (too many turns). '
7. Any favourite Salsa Song?:
'Anything by Van Van. '
8. Any other Comment?:
'The only thing I really dislike about salsa classes is Cuban time. When a class is meant to start at 7, I want it to start at 7 and not 7.45! '

Dancer 13:
1. When did you start to dance Salsa?:
'2002'
2. What interested you to dance Salsa?:
'the music and the culture'
3. Experience while dancing Salsa?:
'good fun'
4. your partner dance Salsa? if not, why?:
'yes'
5. Your experience while dancing La Rueda?:
'good'
6. What style do you prefer? Why?:
'cuban as it is more genuine'
7. Any favourite Salsa Song?:
'valio la pena'
8. Any other Comment?:
''

Dancer 14:
1. When did you start to dance Salsa?:
'1999'
2. What interested you to dance Salsa?:
'loved the dance when I saw it. Used to jive and like couple dancing in general.'
3. Experience while dancing Salsa?:
'nervous to start with and thought it was difficult but used to go home put some salsa music on and kept going over the footwork! turns etc'
4. your partner dance Salsa? if not, why?:
'Not a dance although he wishes he could is very shy in wanting to learn to dance'

Why Salsa?.

5. Your experience while dancing La Rueda?:
'I like Rueda and if done properly its fun and enjoyable'
6. What style do you prefer? Why?:
'I dance on the one with a fusion of LA'
7. Any favourite Salsa Song?:
'LA Luena Negra is the one I still like to hear'
8. Any other Comment?:
"

Dancer 15:
1. When did you start to dance Salsa?:
'11 years ago.'
2. What interested you to dance Salsa?:
'MY husband is cuban.'
3. Experience while dancing Salsa?:
'fun, freedom, connection, exercise.'
4. your partner dance Salsa? if not, why?:
'yes.'
5. Your experience while dancing La Rueda?:
'enjoyment when you get it wright, fun when you get it wrong.'
6. What style do you prefer? Why?:
'1,2,3, pause, as it is the cuban way. I found the tap harder.'
7. Any favourite Salsa Song?:
'I don't understand all the lirics so my taste go with anymusic with a repetetive beat I can hear and follow.'
8. Any other Comment?:
'I haven't danse for a long time and miss it a lot.'

Dancer 16:
1. When did you start to dance Salsa?:
'I started to dance salsa about 5 years ago '
2. What interested you to dance Salsa?:
'The fact that I could go out on my own to a club and not feel left out , as well as the fact I have danced Latin. It just seemed the next best thing without an partner.'
3. Experience while dancing Salsa?:
'Great energy boost, very friendly like minded people and a great way to loose weight and keep fit. '
4. your partner dance Salsa? if not, why?:
'No partner'
5. Your experience while dancing La Rueda?:
'fun when in the right situation. Not so good when the dancers take up most of the floor with a wheel.'
6. What style do you prefer? Why?:
'Cuban. It suites me because , no shines and dancing in a circle with stepping rather than spinning like a top all night. '

Why Salsa?.

7. Any favourite Salsa Song?:
'Lady.'
8. Any other Comment?:
'Where else can a middle aged woman go on her own and feel like she belongs.....Thats Salsa for me.'

Dancer 17:
1. When did you start to dance Salsa?:
'over 10 years ago'
2. What interested you to dance Salsa?:
'the music, the dancing style and fun'
3. Experience while dancing Salsa?:
'a challenge to learn the steps, feel the rhythms and interpret that thru dancing particular salsa styles like Cuban casino. You can make friends. As its partner based, it can also be insightful about people eg the way people relate to dancing, friendly or not, eye contact, fun, politeness etc'
4. your partner dance Salsa? if not, why?:
'No'
5. Your experience while dancing La Rueda?:
'Used to enjoy it not so much now. Don't like the lack of eye contact in the UK and sometimes find it too frantic and clichey'
6. What style do you prefer? Why?:
'Casino. I have tried all salsa styles with many top teachers in London. Dislike dips, triple turns and shines! Too close to ballroom! To me Casino is much nicer for women - funkier, strut the turns, the interpretations are fun-montuno etc and you feel the rhythms more. Plus timba is so rich, complex and sophisticated... fabulous.'
7. Any favourite Salsa Song?:
'so many don't know where to start...'
8. Any other Comment?:
"

Dancer 18:
1. When did you start to dance Salsa?:
'4 years ago'
2. What interested you to dance Salsa?:
'I love to dance'
3. Experience while dancing Salsa?:
'its fullfilled a lot of my dreams'
4. your partner dance Salsa? if not, why?:
'no partner'
5. Your experience while dancing La Rueda?:
'fun'
6. What style do you prefer? Why?:
'like them all prob mambo because as a woman you get more chance to interpretate the music, but like to dance the style of the dance to the music it was meant for'

Why Salsa?.

7. Any favourite Salsa Song?:
'too many'
8. Any other Comment?:
"

Dancer 19:
1. When did you start to dance Salsa?:
'2002'
2. What interested you to dance Salsa?:
'Always liked the music, then my partner started... after a while I thought I'd give it a go'
3. Experience while dancing Salsa?:
'Lot of fun :-)'
4. your partner dance Salsa? if not, why?:
'Yes'
5. Your experience while dancing La Rueda?:
'Love it -- get to dance with everyone'
6. What style do you prefer? Why?:
'Cuban -- more emphasis on enjoyment'
7. Any favourite Salsa Song?:
'Too many to list -- currently "Ain't Nobody" by Alex Wilson'
8. Any other Comment?:
"

Dancer 20:
1. When did you start to dance Salsa?:
'it is the best music there is '
2. What interested you to dance Salsa?:
'the music'
3. Experience while dancing Salsa?:
'keeping fit'
4. your partner dance Salsa? if not, why?:
'has two left feet'
5. Your experience while dancing La Rueda?:
'good fun'
6. What style do you prefer? Why?:
'all'
7. Any favourite Salsa Song?:
"
8. Any other Comment?:
''

Dancer 21:
1. When did you start to dance Salsa?:
'2006'
2. What interested you to dance Salsa?:
'the vibe; culture of dancing; music itself; latine people'
3. Experience while dancing Salsa?:
'love it; makes me smile '

~129~

Why Salsa?.

4. your partner dance Salsa? if not, why?:
'my ex did.'
5. Your experience while dancing La Rueda?:
'don't particularly like it'
6. What style do you prefer? Why?:
'if the partner is a good lead I enjoy any type of salsa/merenge/bachata. as long as he dances 'clean' without trying to grab any parts of my body '
7. Any favourite Salsa Song?:
'marc anthony- many valio la pena (not sure the spelling, sorry) and definately - tu recuerdo the salsa version by ricky martin'
8. Any other Comment?:
'hope salsa/latin thing spreads more not only in the UK but also in Poland/Germany, etc :) '

Dancer 22:
1. When did you start to dance Salsa?:
'1997'
2. What interested you to dance Salsa?:
'I always loved dancing. A friend recommended salsa'
3. Experience while dancing Salsa?:
'Gr8'
4. your partner dance Salsa? if not, why?:
'No partner'
5. Your experience while dancing La Rueda?:
'Gr8'
6. What style do you prefer? Why?:
'Colombian - favourite music, Cuban - most comfortable, LA - most ladies can follow, NY - best for mambo music, Puerto Rican - second fasvourite music'
7. Any favourite Salsa Song?:
'Too many to mention'
8. Any other Comment?:
"

Dancer 23:
1. When did you start to dance Salsa?:
' 17 years ago I accidentally went into a club in Brixton not realising it was salsa! this club was mostly colombian, of course i had no idea how to dance salsa and the colombians were so friendly even tho I speak no spanish! So I promised myself 'ive got to learn this dance'.'
2. What interested you to dance Salsa?:
' I was single and wanted to socialize with the fairer sex! then salsa took over and the ladies were secondary! Until i learned the dance.'
3. Experience while dancing Salsa?:
'what i notice in salsa and it carries on to this day is that an experienced man will dance with a beginner but experienced women will not generally do so. they forget that they were once beginners and if they do not dance with men who are learning then how are they gonna have experienced partners for the future? After all, its just a dance.

Why Salsa?.

Annoyances - when I go somewhere new and ask someone to dance it takes them at least 30 seconds to make up there mind - looking me up from head to toe whether or not they want dance with me. I had the experience one night in a london club of asking 6 different women to dance and got turned down by them because they havent seen me dance before and assumed that because i joined in a lower class than them i can't dance with them. If they say yes after looking me up and down for 30 seconds I put them through the mill! Their expressions are priceless!'

4. your partner dance Salsa? if not, why?:
'oh yes and very good.'

5. Your experience while dancing La Rueda?:
'Not very good at remembering the different names or signs for same moves! Find lots of rueda dancers tend to rush moves and pull people around and when dancing cuban style in couples forget the basic principles of timing.
they think cuban style is just rueda.'

6. What style do you prefer? Why?:
'I learned Cuban and mambo style for 6 years then the LA style came in and I thought this is just another way of getting more money out of us! then realised that i had to do LA style as well. now i've done cuban, miami cuban, la style, mambo style, on 2, puertorican style now when i dance depending on the music i do a combination of all them. but prefer cuban due to the true salsa rythmns.'

7. Any favourite Salsa Song?:
'Desde que no estas - by Rey Ruiz.
and all salsa songs with traditional salsa beats.'

8. Any other Comment?:
'I have, in 17 yrs taken more than 2700 lessons. I know this becos I have kept records- i can see a move and know who first introduced it! What I have noticed in salsa today, the majority - as much as 70-80% of people they want a 'quickfix' - so they dance for a few months and think they are the best. they will not take the time to learn about the music, the dance, all they want to do is moves and do them badly. They fail to realise if you are not dancing to the music you are just going through the motions. I do at least 12hrs every week, i still go to lessons, what annoys me in lessons - guys (and girls)who have been dancing for a few months - the instructor will be showing a move because they recognise a move they just stand there looking bored rather than take the time to listen to the instruction and learn the technique. I am still picking up tips after 17yrs. I still occassionally go into a beginners class /improver/intermediate classes. I sometimes just sit and watch people dancing and realise that as much as 70% are not dancing on the beat and keeping to the tempo. Salsa dancing has not improved infact in the last 4 years it has got worse - possibly due to some teachers who just teach moves without information on timing and technique which they may not even know themselves.

Why Salsa?.

Dancer 24:
1. When did you start to dance Salsa?:
'7 years ago'
2. What interested you to dance Salsa?:
'I have always listened to salsa or found myself in the clubs but could not dance, so I found a class. The rest is history'
3. Experience while dancing Salsa?:
'Freedom, energy, happy, the music is truly a spritual experience '
4. your partner dance Salsa? if not, why?:
'I did have a partner who danced, that's how we meet. I was not as good as he was, I was a beginer he loved to show me the moves! BUT as I got better, more experience, more confident the less he wanted to go out with me!!! WHY?'
5. Your experience while dancing La Rueda?:
'Love it, wish I had more time to learn it.'
6. What style do you prefer? Why?:
'LA'
7. Any favourite Salsa Song?:
'Los Van Van- Soy Todo'
8. Any other Comment?:
'Salsera Para Siempre!'

- STEP 7 – The purpose of a Salsa dancer. (Dance for others).
- STEP 6 – Salsa is a social dance. (Ask for a dance).
- STEP 5 – The Rhythm. (All together).
- STEP 4 – The emotions of the dancer. (Dance happy).
- STEP 3 – The Spirit. (The real dancer).
- STEP 2 – The body of the dancer. (The dance partner of your Spirit).
- STEP 1 – The mind of the dancer. (Mind your mind).

The Seven Spiritual Steps Of Dancing Salsa.

Printed in Great Britain
by Amazon